The Future Testament
Religion Beyond Belief

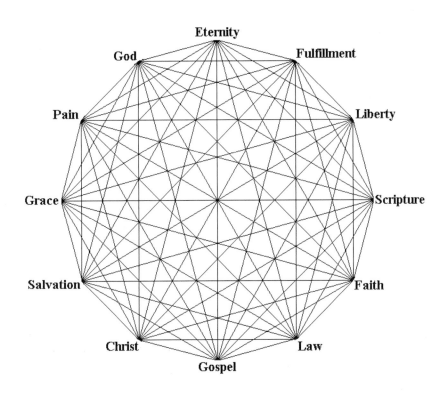

The Future Testament

© 1995 – 2013 by The Church of Yahweh

Published by
The Church of Yahweh
www.Yhwh.com

To every extent possible, this is an original work, though none of us ever live in a vacuum. If you have information to the contrary, please let us know.

The Old Testament and New Testament Bible passages are usually quoted rather freely, often put into our own words. The primary translations referenced are

> The Holy Bible, New International Version®, NIV® Copyright © 1973, 1978, 1984, 2011 by Biblica, Inc.™
>
> New American Standard Bible®, Copyright © 1960, 1962, 1963, 1968, 1971, 1972, 1973, 1975, 1977, 1995 by The Lockman Foundation.
>
> The King James Bible.

Second Revised Edition

International Standard Book Number
978-0-9840792-6-1

www.TheFutureTestament.com

The Future Testament
Table of Contents

Preface i

Introduction: A Very Common Dialogue iii

Covenant xix

Book One: The Book of Fulfillment 1
  Chapter 1 Fruition of the Soul 1
  Chapter 2 Not Old, Not New 4
  Chapter 3 Into the Future 6
  Chapter 4 We Grow, We Learn 9
  Chapter 5 The Essence of It All 13

Book Two: The Book of Liberty 15
  Chapter 1 Systems 15
  Chapter 2 Liberty Is the Heart of God 16
  Chapter 3 Evil Is the Cost of Liberty 17
  Chapter 4 Freedom Within 19
  Chapter 5 Free from Attachments 20
  Chapter 6 The Natural Law 22
  Chapter 7 Proper Governance 24

Book Three: The Book of Scripture 26
  Chapter 1 The Closed Canon 26
  Chapter 2 The Open Canon 27
  Chapter 3 The Fellowship of Religion 29
  Chapter 4 Sacredness 31
  Chapter 5 Reason and Revelation 33
  Chapter 6 Trinity: The Three Are One 35
  Chapter 7 Scripture Equals Knowledge 38
  Chapter 8 A Trinity of Knowledge 40

Book Four: The Book of Faith 42
  Chapter 1 Religion Beyond Belief 42
  Chapter 2 From Belief to Faith to Certainty 43
  Chapter 3 The Scientific Method 45
  Chapter 4 Touching Life 48

Chapter 5 The Power of Faith...51

Book Five: The Book of the Law 53
Chapter 1 Misunderstanding the Law 53
Chapter 2 The Law Is Love 55
Chapter 3 Law Is Harmony..59
Chapter 4 Science and Religion..61
Chapter 5 Connect to the Earth..63

Book Six: The Book of the Gospel...65
Chapter 1 The Crux of the Matter...65
Chapter 2 The Euangeleon..66
Chapter 3 The Good News of Responsibility 67
Chapter 4 Forgiven Christians 70
Chapter 5 Everything Old Is New Again..71
Chapter 6 Resacralization 73
Chapter 7 Life Matters..76

Book Seven: The Book of Christ..78
Chapter 1 The Real Christ 78
Chapter 2 Subject or Object?..79
Chapter 3 Born Again...82
Chapter 4 The Fruit of the Spirit...87
Chapter 5 I Am the Way, the Truth and the Life 88
Chapter 6 Sons and Daughters..90

Book Eight: The Book of Salvation 93
Chapter 1 Beginning Once Again 93
Chapter 2 Discipline and Punishment...95
Chapter 3 True Salvation 97
Chapter 4 Salvation Is Fulfillment..99

Book Nine: The Book of Grace...101
Chapter 1 Ideas Grow and Change 101
Chapter 2 The Old Testament..102
Chapter 3 The New Testament 104
Chapter 4 Humanity Grows Up, a Little..105
Chapter 5 Grace Is Life...107
Chapter 6 Divinity's Children..110

Book Ten: The Book of Pain...113
Chapter 1 The Grace of Pain...113
Chapter 2 Pain the Teacher 114
Chapter 3 The Pitfalls of Avoidance..117

Chapter 4 The Pitfalls of Vengeance.................................... 121
Chapter 5 Two Types of Forgiveness 122
Chapter 6 Love and Pain 124
Chapter 7 Glory to Be Revealed 127

Book Eleven: The Book of God.. 130
Chapter 1 The Changeless Core..................................... 130
Chapter 2 Father God and Mother Nature...................... 132
Chapter 3 The New World 134

Book Twelve: The Book of Eternity................................. 138
Chapter 1 Called to Glory 138
Chapter 2 The Last Words on the Cross 140
Chapter 3 The Second Coming 142
Chapter 4 End Times.. 143
Chapter 5 The Next World.. 145
Chapter 6 Worship 147
Chapter 7 The Breath of God 148

Supplements.. 151
Introduction to the Supplements 152

Supplement 1: Religion and the Scientific Method 153
The Scientific Method.. 155
Recipe, Experience, Community.................................... 157
Religion as Science 158
I Am the Truth... 160
Dogma Abandons Verifiable Knowledge 161
Life Matters... 163
True Religion 164
Mathematics as Bridge.. 165
Assumptions Shape Everything 166
The Two Axioms.. 167
Parables 168

Supplement 2: The Four Aims of Life............................ 170
Money 172
Pleasure 172
Service... 173
God.. 173
Balance and Cooperation 173
Church... 175

Supplement 3: Resacralization....................................... 177

Make Sacred Again..177

Supplement 4: The Ancestral Testaments 181
   For Further Reading...186

Supplement 5: Beyond Biblical Inerrancy........................187
   Small Matters...187
   Matters that Matter...189
   The Truth of God 191

Supplement 6: God's Name Yahweh 193

Supplement 7: Truth in Embryo.......................................196

About the Authors 199

The Future Testament

Preface

A child asks Mommy, "Where do babies come from?" At first the mother says, "When a mommy and daddy love each other, a baby grows in the mommy's tummy." This answer is not wrong. It expresses the essence of a profound truth in a simplified form, one that the child can understand.

An adolescent asks Mom, "Where do babies come from?" The mother says, "Sperm fertilizes the egg." This answer is not wrong. It expresses the essence of a profound truth in a simplified form, one that the adolescent can understand.

Later, the adolescent grows to adulthood, studies molecular biology and nanotechnology and finds answers of wonder completely unimaginable to the child and adolescent.

—\\—

A child-like humanity asks, "How did I get here?" The accepted answer is, "In six days, God made the heavens and the Earth." This answer is not wrong. It expresses the essence of a profound truth in a simplified form, one that the child can understand.

An adolescent humanity asks, "How did I get here?" The answer accepted is, "A big bang materialized all neutrons, protons and electrons, combining for billions of years, generating the physical and life forms you see before you." This answer is not wrong. It expresses the essence of a profound truth in a simplified form, one that the adolescent can understand.

Later, adolescent humanity grows to adulthood, studies mystical cosmology and finds answers of wonder completely unimaginable to the child and adolescent.

—\\—

A child-like humanity asks, "Who was Jesus?" The accepted answer is, "The Son of God." This answer is not wrong. It expresses the essence of a profound truth in a simplified form, one that the child can understand.

An adolescent humanity, a bit more skeptical, asks, "Who was Jesus?" The answer accepted is, "Just a man who taught nice things." This answer is not wrong. It expresses the essence of a profound truth in a simplified form, one that the adolescent can understand.

Later, adolescent humanity grows to maturity and discovers a Jesus of wonder completely unimaginable to the child and adolescent.

—\\—

A child-like humanity asks, "Who wrote scripture?" The accepted answer is, "God wrote the scripture." This answer is not wrong. It expresses the essence of a profound truth in a simplified form, one that the child can understand.

An adolescent humanity, a bit more skeptical, asks, "Who wrote scripture?" The answer accepted is, "Man did, in a quest for understanding." This answer is not wrong. It expresses the essence of a profound truth in a simplified form, one that the adolescent can understand.

Later, adolescent humanity grows to maturity and realizes an answer of wonder completely unimaginable to the child and adolescent.

—\\—

A child-like humanity asks the Father, "What is truth?" At first the Father says, "Thus says the Lord," and the Old Testament is born. This answer is not wrong. It expresses the essence of profound truths in simplified forms, ones that young humanity can understand.

Later, adolescent humanity's elder brother says, "You have heard, but now I say to you…" and the New Testament is born. This answer is not wrong. It expresses the essence of profound truths in simplified forms, ones that the adolescent race can understand.

Much later, adolescent humanity grows to maturity and finds answers of wonder completely unimaginable to the child and adolescent.

And the Future Testament is born.

The Future Testament

Introduction: A Very Common Dialogue

"The Future Testament?" Is this a joke?

No, I assure you, this is not a joke.

You really expect me to believe this is the Future Testament? As in scripture? As in the Bible?

I don't expect you to believe anything. Everything here is different. Everything. As to scripture, that's up to you to decide.

I don't understand a word of that.

Let's start at the beginning. The Old Testament is not "old." It is very much alive and affects the lives of millions of people on the Earth today, both directly and indirectly. And the New Testament is not "new." It is nearly 2,000 years old, and much of it simply does not apply to today.

That's blasphemy. I've always been taught that the Bible, all of it, is the complete, inspired, inerrant and perfect Word of God. To add one word, change one word or remove one word is a sin, and God will punish you with the fires of hell.

Let me ask you a question: Do you believe in slavery?

No, of course not. Slavery is wrong.

I'm glad to hear you say that. But do you even know that the Bible teaches slavery in both the Old and New Testaments? Openly, as an instrument of God. The New Testament actually admonishes:

> "Teach slaves to be subject to their masters in everything, to try to please them, not to talk back to them, and not to steal from them, but to show that they can be fully trusted, so that in every way they will make the teaching about God our Savior attractive."[1]

---

[1] NT Titus 2:9 -10

Notice that slavery is not called an evil to be eliminated, nor an unfortunate part of society to be tolerated, but a tool that God uses in order to advance the Gospel. For the Bible, not only is slavery **acceptable**, but **helpful** in spreading the Gospel.

I'm sure you've taken that out of context.

I'm glad you said that.

You are?

Yes, of course. A disagreement is just fine. A question is wonderful. A doubt is beautiful. You **need** to check things out for yourself and make up your own mind.

I find that so odd. I've been taught all my life that to doubt or question is wrong.

I'm sorry about that. People around you have mistreated you almost all of your life. In your family. In the church. In the government. Even when they are well-intended, the result has been the same: they try to get you to stop thinking for yourself and accept whatever they tell you is true.

Yes, I can see that. Church tells me what I'm supposed to believe, rather than let me question for myself. I was kicked out of Sunday school for asking too many questions. Government tells me to sit back and let them fix my problems. And if I ever questioned my family's traditions, they would disown me.

I am sorry for that, and that's one of the things the Future Testament has come to help with: to encourage you and everyone else to think for themselves. The Bible even tells you to do this:

> "Dear friends, do not believe every spirit, but test the
> spirits to see whether they are from God, because
> many false prophets have gone out into the world."[1]

You see, the **Bible itself** tells you to think, examine and test.

So remember this: everything in this document might be wrong, or at least wrong for you!

---

[1] NT First John 4:1

But, I'm confused... One minute you are quoting something from the Bible as an example of where it is wrong; the next minute you are quoting something that you say is right. What's going on here?

That's a great question. You are paying attention! This is going to be fun.

Fun? I'm not used to thinking about religion as fun.

That's part of what the Future Testament is here to address, my friend. We are made for joy. The Universe exists for the delight and love of all. Of course religion should be fun, just like discovering how chemistry, physics and biology work. Learning and discovery are exciting gifts of God and should be celebrated. There's been too much beating people over the head, forcing them to do, think and believe things they don't want to.

So, speaking of forcing, we were talking about slavery. To repeat, is slavery good or bad?

Of course it's bad.

I agree. Slavery is a horrible practice from when mankind was ignorant and relatively young. But do you realize that in America, literally countless sermons were preached **supporting** slavery on the basis of the **Bible**? Were you taught that those who fought against slavery did so **against the Bible**? Did your church ever inform you that those who fought slavery were called evil because they were trying to "add to" and "take away from" the Bible?

No, I didn't really know that.

Well, it's true. As always, look it up for yourself. Slavery was part of society when the Bible was written, both the Old and New Testaments. Nowhere does the "perfect, inerrant word of God" say that slavery is bad, evil or to be fought. To repeat, it's just the opposite. The Old Testament people were instructed how to **have** slaves, and the New Testament slaves were taught to shut up and **be** good little slaves.

All right, there's no reason to be crude. I don't appreciate talk like that.

I know. It's disgusting. My point is that the entire culture, economy and evil of slavery is supported and encouraged in the "holy" Bible, in context. Check it out for yourself.

I've never heard this. Not in school or church.

I know. The passages that teach slavery have been removed from the yearly liturgical reading cycles, so most good people never hear these things. And most people rarely read the Bible for themselves, so they don't know.

This leads us back to the beginning of our chat. You said, *"I've always been taught that the Bible, all of it, is the complete, inspired, inerrant and perfect Word of God. To add one word, change one word or remove one word is a sin, and God will punish you with the fires of hell."* Well, that "inerrant and perfect" Bible teaches something that in the 21st century we know is wrong and evil. Thousands of Christians gave their lives in America's Civil War, and across the world, in direct opposition to the Bible.

So what are we supposed to do? This is all so confusing.

That's another very good question. People do all kinds of things. Many people try to ignore the problem, saying that slavery back then was different from slavery now, that slavery wasn't all that bad, and all kinds of other rationalizations. Many more go to the opposite extreme, saying that since the Bible supports slavery, it must be an evil (and therefore useless) book.

And what do you say?

I say we need a Future Testament.

Discounting the entire Bible because there are some errors in it is silly. Reputable news sources regularly acknowledge and correct their errors. Only a fool would say the entire news organization was worthless because of some mistakes.

So too, only a fool would say that just because there are problems in the Bible we should ignore the whole thing.

That still just makes me so nervous. "Problems in the Bible?" I've always been taught that was the voice of the devil.

I understand. That thinking comes from an assumption. An assumption is something that is taken for granted or accepted as true without proof. It's a supposition. And the assumption that most of Christianity teaches is that the Bible is perfect, like it was dictated from God Himself.

But the Bible itself says that it is inspired and sent by God, doesn't it?

Yes, there's a passage that says,

> "All scripture is God-breathed and is useful for
> teaching, rebuking, correcting and training in
> righteousness, so that the man of God may be
> thoroughly equipped for every good work."[1]

That passage was written by the same guy (Saint Paul) who said that slaves should be glad to be slaves because it helps spread the Gospel!

Just because something says it is true does not make it true.

But if the whole Bible cannot be counted on as "God-breathed," then how can we tell the difference? How do we tell what is true from what is false? It seems like everyone will be making up their own version of the Bible, deciding their version of truth based on personal feelings.

Lots of excellent points there. We'll take them one at a time.

First, there are **already** many different Bibles. There are many different translations, and while they agree for the most part, sometimes there are significant differences. The details do not matter now, and you can (and should) research them for yourself.

But much more importantly, there are many, many different **interpretations** of the Bible. From these different interpretations come Christianity's hundreds of denominations. At the root of it, what separates the denominations are their interpretations of the Bible: what parts are right and what parts are wrong.

I've never heard of a church talk about the parts of the Bible that are wrong.

Usually it's not said that way. How's this instead: what parts are still right for today, and what parts are not?

OK, now that's more familiar.

The Bible deals with the most challenging material we humans can face. The purpose of life, is there life after death, why is there suffering, how should we live, and so on. But every single word in the Bible was written down by a human being, within a particular time, at a particular place and within a particular culture. So, some of what's written is going to be **eternally** true, while other parts are **culturally** true. That is, they were true for those people there and then but not necessarily true for us here and now.

---

[1] NT Second Timothy 3:16 - 17

That's my point. Like I said, I've always been told that everything in the Bible is eternally true. The "inspired, inerrant, eternal Word of God."

Well, what do you make of slavery?

Ok, you have a point, but what else? Are there other examples?

Have you ever seen a woman in church praying?

Of course.

Did she have her head covered?

What do you mean?

Like a shawl, a scarf, a hat—did she have something on her head?

No, I can't say I've ever seen that.

Well, did she have any hair?

Excuse me?

This lady praying in church with nothing on her head, did she have any hair?

Yes, of course. Are you playing games with me?

I assure you I am not. I am trying to make a point. The Bible says that a woman who prays without her head covered should have her head shaved.[1]

You're kidding.

No, it's there in black and white. What's more, if you read it in context, Saint Paul (the same guy who talks about slaves being quiet) says this is **not** a tradition, but is specifically an **eternal truth**.

So, here's an example of something the Bible itself says is an eternal truth, yet today has been almost universally declared a cultural tradition.

That explains why there are churches where ladies must cover their heads.

That's right. For those people, the passages about covering the head are a part of the eternal truth, not the cultural tradition.

---

[1] NT First Corinthians 11:2 - 11

That's entirely the point. You could go through every verse in the Bible and place an "ET" (**e**ternal **t**ruth) or "CT" (**c**ultural **t**radition) by it. In fact, the various ETs and CTs are exactly what define the denominations. The more ETs, the more orthodox or conservative a group is, and the more CTs, the more reformed or liberal it is.

That's what makes the world go around, as the saying goes.

But that's also the problem—all these different groups with their personal interpretations. Christianity is fractured, all the groups arguing and fighting. That's why I've always been taught that the only way for us to find peace is for everyone to accept everything as the Word of God, as literal truth. To use your terms, every verse should have an ET by it.

Very well stated. But first, those who say they accept the "whole Bible, and nothing but the Bible," no matter how ultra-orthodox, are lying to themselves.

Excuse me?

There is not one person on the Earth, not a single person, who accepts every single verse of the Bible as true, and lives by it.

Oh really?

Yes, really. Most of the time they cannot even see this themselves. They will teach and preach that the Bible is perfect in every word and that every word must be followed; they will express disdain, even hatred, for those who do not believe as they do. Yet those people always ignore parts of the Bible.

Like what?

Like loving your enemies and praying for those who persecute you. Like not borrowing anything and owing nothing to anyone, and so on. There are literally thousands of church buildings housing Biblical literalist groups, with hundreds of thousands of dollars on the mortgage. Yet Saint Paul clearly says that we must "owe **nothing** to **anyone** except the debt of love."[1] This is just one example of how people do not see that they themselves are guilty of the very thing they condemn others for. I could give many other examples.

---

[1] NT Romans 13:8

The central point is this: Those who **say** we should accept the entire Bible, every word of it, **don't**. No one does. Not one single person, anywhere.

So, either by teaching or practice, everyone has **some** cultural traditions invisibly indicated in their Bible's liner notes.

That's why they say the church is full of hypocrites.

I do not see it that way. Most of the time people are just not aware of what they are doing, or everything the Bible says, or both.

You see, most people do not even work as hard on their religion as we have worked here in this little chat. By "work on religion" I mean to think, use logic, search their hearts, consider, get all the facts and make decisions. Almost everyone on the Earth has exactly the same religion. There are about a billion Christians, about a billion Muslims, about a billion Hindus and so on, but the overwhelming majority of people (estimates world-wide are as high as 95%) have **exactly the same religion**. Care to take a guess what that religion is?

Deism? Humanism? I have no idea.

The answer is: whatever Mommy and Daddy tell me is true. Christians give birth to Christians. Muslims give birth to Muslims. Hindus give birth to Hindus, on and on, through all the sections of the symphony that is the human race.

So, you see, most people are not so much hypocrites as they are unaware. Their religion is something that was given to them, inherited through birth, just like their language, the country they live in or hair color. There are many reasons for this. For the most part, children are born to parents who inherited their religion from **their** parents. So, questioning that religion is tantamount to doubting one's entire social support system. This can be a risky thing. Thus is born blind acceptance, obedience, and from it, prejudice: people may not have examined their own inherited religion much (if at all), but they "know" theirs is true and everyone else's is wrong.

And that's what we call "religion" for most of the planet in the 21st century. Another reason for the Future Testament is to call people to examine their own religions.

It is time to get serious about the planet, the totality of humanity, and therefore our individual religions.

Again, most people are simply unaware of the details of the texts they consider holy and perfect. Likewise, most people are unaware of the ways their own lives are out of touch with said text. It's not so much hypocrisy as ignorance.

OK, I can see that, but it really doesn't help. I mean, if the Bible is not completely perfect and cannot be trusted, how can we tell the parts that are true from false? How can we separate the eternal truths from the cultural traditions?

Once again, most people never ask, let alone answer this question. The fact that you are reading this makes you a special person. Almost everyone accepts their eternal truths and cultural traditions by default, as a part of the religion they inherit from their parents.

All right, I can see that. But that doesn't answer the question. Assuming that I want to separate the ETs from the CTs (I can't believe I'm talking like this!) what do I do?

Welcome to the Future Testament.

I don't understand. Could you help a bit?

The challenge of a genuine, aware, religious life is to distinguish eternal truth from cultural tradition within scriptures and denominations. Then, with the eternal truths firmly identified, determine the best way to express those timeless realities today, here and now, within *this* time, place, language and culture, to create a new tradition.

The Future Testament is here to help do that. Just like Jesus did not come to abolish the Old Testament but to fulfill it, (to re-establish its eternal truths in the different world of his day) the Future Testament has not come to abolish the New Testament but to fulfill it.[1]

Part of the Future Testament examines the Old and New Testaments in the light of the 21st century. Inside the castle of faith, things are not very much different from where they were in the Dark Ages. Meanwhile, outside the castle we are splitting atoms, performing laser eye surgery, doing genetic DNA manipulation and categorizing dark holes in the center of billions of galaxies. Certainly, we are way overdue for a serious reexamination of the eternal truths and cultural traditions of scripture.

---

[1] FT Fulfillment 2:2

This process need not be painful, though it is challenging. Consider all the blood that was shed over changing slavery from an eternal truth to a cultural tradition. Ideas do not change quickly, especially those that are the least examined. In other words, the more a religious idea is a part of one's subconscious inheritance, the harder it is to examine objectively, and thus change. In point of fact, it was easier for humanity to split the atom than it was to say the Bible was wrong about slavery.

Why the "Future" Testament?

We do not delude ourselves that the Future Testament will be widely accepted at this point in time. Hatred flows deep, prejudice runs wide, and religious ignorance and bigotry have advanced little from the Crusades and witch burnings of centuries gone by. So, the "Future" part of the Future Testament is a note of hope that the view of eternal truths embodied in this scripture will be accepted ever more widely as time goes forth.

"Scripture" has always meant the Word of God. So you are saying this is now the Word of God?

Maybe, maybe not.

You're not helping.

I'm trying to. Whether the Future Testament, written at the dawn of the 21st century A.D., is scripture or not is up to you.

You see, everything is different. **Everything**. The Old Testament was written on sheepskin. The New Testament was written on papyrus. The Future Testament was written with a word processing program on a personal computer running on electricity.

The Old and New Testaments have literally been forced down people's throats, demanding they be accepted on pain of death. The Future Testament states, very clearly and up front, that truth or falsehood can be determined by you, the individual reader, **and you alone**. Physically forcing someone to do anything is a part of humanity's animalistic past. True love, the end goal of humanity's pathway, requires each person to be endowed with complete freedom. That includes making up your own mind about religion, and in particular the Old, New and Future Testaments.

Yes, the Future Testament presents ideas, many of them. It also offers a significant reevaluation of ETs and CTs, in the light of a post-nuclear world.

But much more than that, it provides a new method, a new way of **approaching** religion, and thus your very soul.

In days of old, people were (and are) forced to accept things as true that could not be explained or justified, but nevertheless must be accepted. The Future Testament is different. Instead of demanding blind allegiance to creeds that cannot be explained, let alone justified, the Future Testament invites you to escape your cultural prejudices and think for yourself.

Is the Future Testament "**scripture**?" That's for you to decide.

You are born on the Earth, and Yahweh says (though this message is often drowned out by the noise of society), "You are free. Free to go where you will, seek and find what you will."[1] Of course there are dangers,[2] but our free will is not an illusion. It is a Divine Gift.

So, in the ways of old, when people were (are) forced into any belief system, that in and of itself violates Yahweh's Heart. You are free. Really, truly, infinitely free, more free than you can presently imagine. That freedom extends to the Future Testament: you are free to seek it, free to ignore it *and* free to find Yahweh's Word here. The Future Testament honors your mind, your heart and all the gifts of God that are yours not by cultural, but by **Divine** birthright.

So, what, is this channeling God?

No, absolutely not.

Everything here is different. Everything. The Future Testament was written by people, just people (So were the Old and New Testaments, but your culture does not want you to know that). We have parents and our own history, and we are very much human. We are even prone to misunderstanding, and will admit that up front.

There is no "Thus says the Lord" here. You are free to find the eternal Word of God here, or not. How you respond to the Future Testament is your choice.

---

[1] OT Genesis 2:16
[2] OT Genesis 2:17

The Future Testament is no "channeling" of God. That's a cute idea, but it just does not work that way. Throughout time, people seek for and reach out to God. God answers the questions the best way the seeker can understand. But the Infinite is always, at best, filtered through our finite understanding, or lack of it.

Don't be shocked that there are new ideas here. You do not have to accept any of them; you do not have to be afraid. No one can now be, nor ever be, *forced* to accept anything here as true.

But there *are* new ideas here. As such, the Future Testament is a part of a long tradition of religious wisdom. Different parts of the Old Testament correct other parts of the Old Testament.[1] Jesus corrects parts of the Old Testament.[2] Different writers in the New Testament disagree with each other.[3] That's ok, too. The Future Testament tries to add its voice to that dialogue.

Sorry, but that still reeks of blasphemy to me.

Just what part?

I don't know exactly. Just the idea of scripture being written by a person, correcting the Bible. I mean, who are you? Who appointed you to do this?

We are just people. No one appointed us to do this. We have sought for God with all our hearts and minds for decades. We have pondered the deepest questions and sought how we should practically live. The results, our answers, we have written for all the world to see.

Some have found our observations to be blasphemy. That is entirely understandable. Others have found, well, it's hard to put into words. Let's put it like this: they have found perspectives and ideas that have answered questions they have wondered about their entire lives, with more clarity than they have found anywhere else.

It is for those people that we write. That is the "testament" part of the Future Testament. As citizens of the 21st century, this is our testament to the truths of the Universe as we understand them.

---

[1] OT Amos 5:21, OT Hosea 6:6, FT Supplement 5 - Beyond Biblical Inerrancy
[2] NT Matthew 19:8
[3] NT James 2:20

The "future" part of the Future Testament is a prayer of hope, that the ideas here might grow, organically, voluntarily and without violence, to be an ever-greater part of human consciousness.

Ideas like what? Can you summarize?

The Future Testament can be summarized in five little words:

Our ideas are too small.

What ideas?

ALL our ideas, my friend. Our ideas about the size of the Universe, until just a few years ago, were like comparing a pea to a mountain. Our ideas about the complexity of matter, likewise, were (are) nowhere near the full truth. So too our ideas about God are way too small. Likewise, our ideas about ourselves, life after death, Jesus, the Gospel, salvation and scripture (just to name a few) are all too small. The truth, the real truth, (as much as we are able to understand at the beginning of the 21st century) is vast, glorious and mind-bogglingly transcendent, literally beyond our wildest comprehension.

Most of our current popular religions, compared to the vision of the Future Testament, are like counting on your fingers compared to the fastest super computer.

That's a pretty bold statement. So you think you know all this? Why should we trust you?

Thank you, I love you, and I love that question! The answer is, **you should not, MUST NOT, trust us**. Everything here is different. **Everything**. In days of old, you were forced to accept what you were told, just because the person had authority or power. The Future Testament is entirely different. You are not expected to accept or believe **any** of it. In fact, this document demands that you do NOT accept or believe any of it without **testing it for yourself**.

Do **not** trust us. Do **not** mindlessly believe a single word of the Future Testament. Accept nothing here. Read it, consider it, examine it. Accepting something, **anything**, someone else tells you just because you think they have some form of authority, is one of the worst things you can do for your soul. The only thing worse is never looking or asking at all.

But here is an admonition: if you are looking through the Future Testament just to see if it matches what you already think is true, we suggest you not waste your time. Assume (it's a good bet) that very little here will match your current views. So let's just say this is blasphemy and pointless delusion, okay?

So let's see if I understand your position.

Please.

The Bible is not a mathematically perfect book. We need to separate the eternal truths from cultural traditions, like slavery. The Future Testament is one such reexamination, though it is not a "channeling" or any other "New Age" mumbo-jumbo. As Jesus came to fulfill the Old Testament, the Future Testament has come to fulfill the New Testament. And the Future Testament itself demands that we not accept or believe any of this?

That's exactly right! You have it!

So you are going to tell us what we really should believe?

No, absolutely not.

Let me rephrase that. You are going to give us newer, better beliefs?

No, absolutely not. The Future Testament is not a different system of beliefs. Everything is different here. Everything.

The Future Testament offers Religion Beyond Belief.

You're kidding.

Again, I assure you I am not. In the 21st century we are ready to move into the next stage of religious thought, and that means going beyond arguing about different beliefs, until we enter the realm of knowledge.

That will take quite some explanation.

I realize that. That's what we're here for.

The Future Testament is not just a collection of new ideas. New ideas are indeed a part, but a much more essential aspect of the Future Testament is that it provides you with a brand new way of **approaching** religion.

Remember, everything here is different. Everything:

The ways of old demand unquestioning
acceptance of antiquated ideas.
The Future Testament demands that you question
everything, including itself.

The ways of old stop at mindless belief,
except for threats of punishment for non-conformity.
The Future Testament presents an
entirely different way of approaching religion:
Religion Beyond Belief.

This new approach is as radical and revolutionary
as any specific idea presented.

We hope you will join us.

The Future Testament

Covenant

In the Old Testament, Yahweh made a covenant with Abraham, Isaac and Jacob to be His chosen people.
In the New Testament, Yahweh made a covenant with the whole human race, through salvation in Jesus the Christ.
Here in the Future Testament *you* have the opportunity to make a covenant with yourself and the whole of humanity.
You will find many ideas here. Some you may like, some you may not. You are free to react to the Future Testament exactly and precisely as you choose. You may ignore it; you might hate it.

But if you love the Future Testament and what you
find here, then the covenant you make with yourself
and the whole world is to never use what you find here
as a tool to hate or harm another, or even to think or
feel less of them.

No one can ever be coerced into reading the Future Testament.
No one can ever be forced to embrace any of its ideas.
No one can ever be threatened with loss of fellowship, excommunication or the fires of hell for not resonating with the Future Testament.

As you are free to love it, others are free to hate it.

And if you are one of those who find the Future Testament a blessing in your life, this is the covenant you *must* make.

It is the only requirement.

Welcome to
the Future Testament

This book is dedicated to
all the future generations
of the human race, in the hope
that it might help them find
their fulfillment of life and love,
as complete incarnations
of the living God.

The Future Testament

Book One: The Book of Fulfillment

Chapter 1
Fruition of the Soul

1 In the end there will be fulfillment.

2 The Old Testament begins, "In the beginning God created the heavens and the Earth."[1]

3 The New Testament says, "In the beginning was the Word, and the Word was with God, and the Word was God."[2]

4 The Future Testament begins with prayer for the fulfillment of each individual soul and hope for the perfection of the entire human race.

5 It is often good to begin at the end.

6 When people lose sight of the goal, they lose their way.

7 Your life has a purpose, a goal, a reason for existing: God's Plan is for Christ to be formed in you.[3]

8 When Christ is formed in you, then you are a temple of the Holy Spirit.

9 When the Holy Spirit lives in you, it bears fruit, like lush oranges and apples on trees.

---

[1] OT Genesis 1:1
[2] NT John 1:1
[3] NT Galatians 4:19

10 The fruit of the Spirit[1] is the fruition of your soul:

> The **Love** of God, which is the only Law.[2]
> **Joy** to you and the whole world.[3]
> The **Peace** of God which passes understanding.[4]
> **Patience** to both wait and work for others' fulfillment.[5]
> **Kindness** expressed by God to us, which we show to the world.[6]
> **Goodness**, as every thing was created, *very* good.[7]
> The **Faith** which, as a mustard seed, will move mountains.[8]
> **Gentleness**, tender affection for all those who hurt.[9]
> **Self-control**, the Heart of God: "I will be what I will to be."[10]

11 The Future Testament is here to aid the fruition of your personal soul, and the fulfillment of all humanity.

12 Fulfillment is Yahweh's promise; it is both your personal calling and the destiny of the human race.

13 Individual fulfillment will echo throughout the collective human race, becoming united as one body, the Bride of Christ,[11] eternally one with the Holiness of Yahweh.

14 As the cells in your body work together to house your spirit, so too each human will become one cell in the literal Body of Christ.

15 Life! Excitement! We are called to the eternal celebration of all creation!

16 The Future Testament invites you to an ever-deepening fulfillment of satisfaction, warmth, love and goodness.

17 Love, knowledge, growth and true fulfillment go on forever, for God is infinite.

18 Lessons learned need not be re-learned, and the Future Testament looks to the time when humanity has learned the lessons of its youth. But never think of the Future Testament as a *final* testament.

---

[1] NT Galatians 5:22
[2] NT Matthew 22:37 - 40
[3] NT Luke 2:10
[4] NT Philippians 4:7
[5] NT Hebrews 6:12
[6] OT Hosea 11:4
[7] OT Genesis 1:31
[8] NT Matthew 17:20
[9] NT Colossians 3:12
[10] OT Exodus 3:14
[11] NT First Corinthians 12:27; Ephesians 4:12

19 It is our expressed prayer that the truths contained herein will be the living experience of the human race as it grows to its glorious future.
20 At the dawn of the 21st century, it is clear we still have a long journey ahead.
21 The Future Testament is here to help you find fulfillment on a continual basis, as life expresses a joyous unfolding of Yahweh's purpose, for your life and all those around you.
22 Consider the twelve books of the Future Testament as a united invitation:

An invitation to explore the
Fulfillment of your destiny.
An invitation to celebrate the glorious
Liberty which is your divine birthright.[1]
An invitation to find all existence
to be your sacred **Scripture.**[2]
An invitation to experience **Faith**
as life-changing assurance and confidence.[3]
An invitation to discover the
love of Yahweh's **Law.**[4]
An invitation to live the transformation
which is the heart of the genuine **Gospel.**
An invitation to find **Christ** forming in you,
the mystery of the ages.[5]
An invitation to touch and feel the
sweetness of perfected **Salvation.**[6]
An invitation to experience each moment
as an expression of **Grace.**[7]
An invitation to learn from **Pain,**
and see it as a kind teacher.[8]
An invitation to **God**'s Eternal Glory,
which is your true calling,[9]
An invitation that rings through all **Eternity.**[10]

---

[1] OT Genesis 2:15
[2] OT Psalm 19:1
[3] NT Hebrews 11:1
[4] NT Romans 7:12
[5] NT Colossians 1:27
[6] OT Isaiah 12:3
[7] NT Second Corinthians 9:8
[8] NT Romans 8:18
[9] NT First Peter 5:10
[10] OT Ecclesiastes 3:11

Chapter 2
Not Old, Not New

1 Jesus and the New Testament did not come to *abolish* the Old Testament, but to *fulfill* it.

2 In exactly the same way, the Future Testament has not come to *abolish* the Gospel, but to *fulfill* it.

3 The Old Testament was a gift of God.

4 But the "Old" Testament is not really *old*. Its ideas continue to inspire us. The revelation of God's sacred name "Yahweh" continues to convey power and wonder, thousands of years after Moses climbed Mount Sinai.

5 The essential relationship of God as Father remains central to our religious devotion.

6 Even today the Old Testament stories motivate millions. The stories of Abraham, Isaac, Ishmael, and Jacob, and the covenant that Yahweh made with them, create geopolitical forces that shape the lives of nations.

7 The Exodus from slavery remains a perfect model of newfound freedom for multitudes, a living embodiment of the challenges we all face when seeking release from bondage.

8 The Torah's legal system remains the model of western justice. Most of the laws established in the Old Testament, especially the Ten Commandments, remain at the heart of our legal system.

9 Even Deuteronomy's structure, with a preamble, precepts and punishments, is the way the majority of our legal documents are structured.

10 The Old Testament prophets wisely warned that immorality leads to destruction. Their admonitions centuries ago remain as relevant today as when uttered.

11 Much more than that, the Old Testament's traditions and events, especially Passover and the Exodus from Egypt, became the foundation of the New Testament.

12 The Future Testament reveres the divine revelation of Yahweh's Law and the words of wisdom spoken by His prophets to the people of Israel.

13 To appreciate the New Testament, it is essential to have a deep understanding of the Old Testament.

14 The New Testament likewise was a gift of God.

15 In the Old Testament, we learned of God as Father. In the New Testament, we learned of God as one of us.

16 The Future Testament affirms the strength, power, glory, revelation and necessity of salvation through faith in Christ, as written in the New Testament. Millennia after Christ's death, we are still barely able to comprehend what that means.

17 But the New Testament is not really *new*. It was written 2000 years ago in a world stranger than most of us can possibly imagine: no cars, television, radio, electricity, computers or penicillin.

18 Each technological revolution brings moral and religious challenges.

19 Politics, monetary systems, communication and science, even what *religion* itself means, have changed in countless ways since the New Testament was *new*.

20 Retaining the essential core of eternal truth, while all around society undergoes drastic revolution, requires diligent application of an open heart and mind.

21 The Future Testament is a part of the great stream of consciousness which has led from the Old to the New, into today.

22 To understand the New Testament, it is essential to have an understanding of the Old Testament.

23 Likewise, in order to have a deep understanding of the Future Testament, it is essential to understand both the Old and the New Testaments.

> We recognize both the Old and New Testaments
> as containing infinite truth in embryo,
> seeds of deep truth planted in order to
> grow the vine of humanity
> and to eventually reap the harvest.
> The Future Testament seeks to help
> fulfill both the Old and New Testaments
> by showing deeper, enhanced appreciations
> of their glory and value.
> From the Old to the New, into the Future.

24 As Jesus did not come to *abolish* the Law, but *fulfill* it, so too the Future Testament has not come to *abolish* the Gospel, but to *fulfill* it.

Chapter 3
Into the Future

1 For many people, the most sacrilegious notion about this book is that it exists at all.

2 Those people will find the idea of a Future Testament to be abhorrent because, for them, Yahweh's sacred book *The Holy Bible* is complete and perfect.

3 For many, God said everything the human race needed to know thousands of years ago, through the Law, Prophets, Gospel and Apostles. To add or change one word[1] is, for them, blasphemy.

4 The Future Testament refers to misunderstandings in classical Christian theology as "the ways of old."

5 For those who cling insistently to the ways of old, if something agrees with the Bible, then it need not be stated, for it is redundant. On the other hand, if something *dis*agrees with the Bible, then clearly it must be wrong, and is therefore evil.

6 If you find your church, faith, community, worldview, holy books and religion completely satisfying, then the Future Testament is simply not for you. Put it down. Do not waste your time.

7 The Future Testament is entirely optional.

8 No one will be forced into reading this book. No one will be coerced into learning the Future Testament. There will be no religion formed around it. No one will ever kneel at the foot of a soldier and be put to death for not giving his or her assent to the Future Testament.

9 Force and coercion are completely against the Heart of God, and utterly against everything the Future Testament stands for.[2]

10 The Future Testament has been written because, for millions of people, the ways of old simply fail to express relevance in our modern technological world.

11 Eternal truths forever stay the same, the very definition of "eternal." But the ways in which these eternal truths are *understood* and *expressed* need to be continually reevaluated in light of cultural change.

---

[1] NT Revelation 22:18 & 19
[2] FT Liberty 2:14

12 If you are not convinced, that's perfectly fine. No judgment, no grudges, no one will think less of you. We do not wish to be offensive or threatening.

13 Maybe you will never find any of this material valuable, and that is fine with us.

14 If you ever choose to examine it, we hope that you live in a society where you are free to experience this book in your own way, at your own pace, in your own time.

15 The castle of the church stands crumbling, holding desperately onto the ways of old, reciting the same creeds and understandings that were little more than political compromises hundreds of years ago. Meanwhile, all around the castle, society has so completely changed that the ways of old are increasingly challenged to express relevance.

16 We know so much more about the physical Universe now than we could even imagine 100 short years ago. We live in a world where knowledge has been able to transform itself into technologies that were *unimaginable* 100 years ago.

17 In our era of atom-smashing devices, of telescopes that have catalogued billions of galaxies, of DNA manipulation and one-world communication technologies, we are forced to reconsider:

How do we relate to each other?
How do we find our fulfillment?
What does "God" mean?
What does it mean to find Old Testament Law
fulfilled in such a world without
falling into the pitfalls of fascism?
How do we fulfill the Gospel,
saving it from being relegated to
an antiquated belief system?
How do we discern Eternal Scriptural Truth
from cultural tradition?
And, perhaps most challenging of all,
how do we find and express
God's Spirit of immutable Love
in our ever-changing technological era?

18 Helping you find your own answers to these questions is the purpose of the Future Testament.

19 At its heart, religion is a quest for the Eternal Truths of God, which stand separate and apart from all temporal considerations.

20 God is, indeed, the same yesterday, today and forever.[1]

21 We are challenged by the Spirit to rise above the cultural noise around us, to find that which is eternally true, transcending space and time.

22 Our understanding of the world and how we relate to it (our culture, governmental systems, technologies, cosmologies and sciences) are always changing.

23 In order to discover eternal truth, the *processes* by which we look for it must grow and evolve.

24 How do we find and apply Yahweh's infinite, eternal, timeless truths to the ever-changing cultural timeframe in which we find ourselves?

25 We cannot find God in the same ways we did 2,000 years ago. Desert sacrifices do not convey the same meaning they once did; now they are called barbeques.

26 We cannot even *look for Him* in the same way we did 2,000 years ago. Now 40 days in the desert is called a luxury vacation.

27 But *change need not threaten faith.*

28 Technology can serve and extend the reach of the Spirit.

29 Advances in science should further our knowledge of the Divine.

30 Every scientific fact, every mathematical discovery, can add to the wellspring of inspiration from which we draw the parables of the Universe.

31 Jesus' parables were about seeds and fish. Our third millennium parables[2] are about fractals, cars, computers and $e=mc^2$.

32 Expanding knowledge of the physical Universe will be our ascending guide into the blissful realms of the Spirit.

---

[1] OT Malachi 3:6
[2] FT God Chapter 3

Chapter 4
We Grow, We Learn

1 As above, so below: the growth that an individual experiences is reflected in the group, and vice versa.

2 Individuals and groups begin with very simple, concrete ideas; they mature into more complex, symbolic thought.

3 You can actually see many ideas develop (change) within the Old and New Testaments.

4 The Future Testament hopes to be part of that great tradition.

5 The Future Testament invites you to think differently (the original meaning of "repent") about many things.

6 The Old Testament notion of "law" meant strict obedience, or certain punishment. The Future Testament wants to fulfill the Law by showing people a different way of looking at it.

7 Jesus fulfilled the Old Testament Law by living it. There were parts of the Law that he needed to improve because people had become wiser and circumstances had changed. For example, Jesus enhanced the peoples' understanding of divorce[1] and the Sabbath.[2]

8 Learn the Law of love:

> The Law is fulfilled
> when we realize
> we are not punished
> *for* our sins,
> but we are punished
> *by* our sins.

9 God did not establish arbitrary rules and tests that would trap us in disobedience.[3]

10 Rather, Yahweh was giving us warnings and divine guidance as to how we can best live our lives, so we can reach fulfillment.

11 Jesus said, "I have come that you might have life, and that more abundantly."[4].

12 Jesus' notion of abundant life includes supreme celebrations, great feasts and peak experiences shared by all.

---

[1] NT Matthew 5:31
[2] NT Matthew 12
[3] FT Liberty 3:4 - 6, Salvation 1:6 - 12
[4] NT John 10:10

13 Jesus' abundant life included his fulfilled notion of the Law: the heart of the Law is to love God with all your being and love your neighbors as yourself. Jesus lived this, and invites us to do the same.[1]
14 The Law is *not* an enemy. The Law is Love. Love is the Law.
15 Jesus enhanced the peoples' understanding of what the prophets meant in some of their writings: for example, what it means to be "*ha'mashiach*," the Messiah, the Anointed One, the Christ.
16 He challenged the notions of the entire nation about who the Messiah was and what He would do.
17 Jesus was constantly enhancing people's understandings, correcting them where necessary. And his life was consistent with what he taught.
18 Jesus gave a renewed sense of warm, glowing wonder to the Old Testament Law and Prophets. He didn't come to end the Law or the Prophets. He came to manifest, in human form, the beauty and glory of what was introduced in the Old Testament.
19 The Future Testament invites *you* to be the manifestation of the beauty and glory of what was introduced in the New Testament.
20 Jesus came that we might find our lives *fulfilled*—not completed, not finished or stopped, but made *whole*.
21 When your life is fulfilled, your life is not at an end.
22 You need not wait until death to find fulfillment; those who say you do are well intended, but grievously in error.
23 Fulfillment here on Earth, living a peace-filled, complete life, is indeed possible; in fact, it is God's promise.[2]
24 The Future Testament will show that Yahweh's plan for each of us is to experience fulfillment while *alive*, just as Jesus demonstrated.

What does fulfillment look like?
What does it feel like?
What does it smell like?
How do we know when we have it?
What does it mean to follow Christ
in a post-nuclear age?

25 The Gospel is not a set of ideas (doctrines) that we have to agree with in our "confessions of faith" to be forgiven by God.
26 *Real* salvation is ever so much more than simply being forgiven.
27 The Future Testament will show the joys of living not just a Christ-*centered* life but also a Christ-*conscious* life.

---

[1] NT Matthew 22:35 - 40
[2] NT First Peter 5:10

28 The Future Testament seeks to fulfill the Gospel, helping us to take up our crosses and follow Christ.

29 Our true salvation lies in *being as he is.*[1]

30 As the scripture says, "Let the same mind be in you that was in Christ Jesus."[2] And, "Everyone, after he has been fully instructed, *will be like his teacher.*"[3]

31 The Future Testament wants to help show you how to be like our teacher.

32 Yahweh's Holy Spirit has been planted in us, just like a seed planted in the ground:

> A seed needs to die to its individual isolation,
> grow roots in the Earth,
> get enough water to reach into the sky,
> spreading its branches toward the Sun and,
> with healthy air, clean water,
> good nutrients in the Earth
> and radiant sunlight,
> the tree will eventually bear fruit.
> The seeds contained within the fruit
> will give life to a million generations.

33 This is a living parable of your spiritual life. The process shows the fulfillment of both the seed and the tree.

34 Seed, tree, forest. One.

35 Spirit, incarnation, humanity. One.

36 The fruit of the Spirit is the fulfillment of your soul. One fruit, with many aspects, just as one orange has many characteristics.

37 The Old, New and Future Testaments seek individual salvation *and* the fulfillment of the entire human race. For indeed, like a hand in a glove and a glove on a hand, the two work together.

38 Society cannot be fulfilled until its individual citizens are fulfilled, but no citizen can realize their true destiny as long as society remains full of pain, suffering, anguish and war.

39 We are all connected.

40 We are all in this together.

41 True fulfillment is the conscious presence of Yahweh's Infinite Spirit in every human heart and mind:

---

[1] FT Salvation 3:17 - 23
[2] NT Philippians 2:5
[3] NT Luke 6:40

Individually,
in every home,
in every corporation,
in every nation
and in the entire planet.

42 Personal and societal salvation work hand in hand.

43 As individuals, we have to become Spirit-filled for society to come to fruition.

44 The harvest is for the whole world.

45 The entire social order will exhibit the fruit of the Spirit: love, joy, peace, patience, kindness, goodness, faithfulness, gentleness and self-control.

46 Christ in the flesh, building the Body of Christ.

47 Every individual is a part of a group, and every group is made up of its individuals.

48 "One for all and all for one" is literally, scientifically, economically, religiously and experientially true.

49 As long as individuals continue to selfishly strive, at the expense of others, they cannot have the fruit of the Spirit.

50 The society in which cruel selfishness resides cannot be considered fulfilled.

Chapter 5
The Essence of It All

1 The essence of it all, from the perspective of the Future Testament, is this:

Our ideas are too small.

2 Our religious ideas are too small.
3 Our ideas about God are too small.
4 Our ideas about ourselves, our world and the Universe are too small.
5 In exactly the same way we have learned that the physical Universe is infinitely larger than previously imagined…that the structures of the cell are vastly more intricate than Darwin could ever have guessed… that the family of subatomic particles is more complex than we can conceive…
6 The Future Testament declares that our religious ideas are too small.

Our ideas about **Fulfillment** are too small.
Our ideas about **Liberty** are too small.
Our ideas about **Scripture** are too small.
Our ideas about **Faith** are too small.
Our ideas about **Law** are too small.
Our ideas about the **Gospel** are too small.
Our ideas about **Christ** are too small.
Our ideas about **Salvation** are too small.
Our ideas about **Grace** are too small.
Only our ideas about our personal **Pain** are too *large*.
Our ideas about **God** are all too small.
Our ideas about **Eternity** are too small.

7 The radical transformations occurring on this planet are not only happening politically, economically, technologically and scientifically.
8 The renaissance in the realms of quantum physics, biology, cosmology and astronomy *is likewise happening in the realms of religion.*
9 The Bible itself hinted at this revolution. Jesus spoke of "having many things to say" but said that we were unable to bear them.[1]

---

[1] NT John 16:12

10 Perhaps now, with all that we've learned about our Father's Creation, we are positioned to be able to understand some of Jesus' "many things."

11 Perhaps, just perhaps, our DNA-weaving, laser-beam wielding society is ready to learn some of the meatier things of the Word.[1]

12 For as Jesus said, "You shall know the truth and the truth shall make you free."[2]

13 The Future Testament is here to help expand your notions of religious truth.

14 In order to have knowledge, you must have freedom.

15 In order to have freedom, you must have knowledge.

16 Love of God, love of people. One.

17 Fulfillment of the one, fulfillment of the many.

18 Hand and glove. The two are one. One system. Learn the lesson well.

---

[1] NT Hebrews 5:12
[2] NT John 8:32

The Future Testament

Book Two: The Book of Liberty

Chapter 1
Systems

1 Our ideas about liberty are too small.

2 Jesus said, "You shall know the truth and the truth shall set you free."[1]

3 Truth breeds freedom, which in turn generates knowledge. They work together, as a system. The two are not one flesh,[2] but one *system*.

4 Knowledge and freedom are equal partners in the service of true salvation.

5 We live in a world of systems: every effect has a cause, and causes are themselves an effect. It is not that we first gain knowledge which then leads to freedom; rather, knowledge and freedom grow together, like your left and right hands coordinate to serve you.

6 Too often we explore ideas in isolation, blind to the astounding interconnectedness of the Universe.

7 Body and soul, meaning and language, child and family, finance and spirit: these are *systems* that consist of interdependent elements, which only find their true value in the presence of what surrounds them.

8 Expand your understanding of freedom: in your quest for the perfect fulfillment of your life, you are free to explore *everything*.

9 You have the freedom to learn everything there is to know about yourself, God and the infinite cosmos.

10 Celebrate your liberty: learn *everything* about *everything*.

11 Liberty is primal. Without the freedom to read, learn and explore, you will be seriously hindered in what you can *know*.

12 Like branches and leaves on a tree, truth and liberty grow together or not at all.

---

[1] NT John 8:32
[2] OT Genesis 2:24

Chapter 2
Liberty Is the Heart of God

1 Liberty is the heart of Yahweh's nature, the Universe, and His plan for us.

2 Liberty is even reflected as the essence of God's Name.

3 God's sacred Name "Yahweh," as revealed in the Old Testament,[1] literally means "I will be what I will be," or "I will be what I choose to be." This name embodies the formula that generates all existence:

$$I + Will = Being$$

4 Will, as in free will, as in "I, the God of the Universe, have the liberty to do as I choose. My willing generates the Universe of all being."

5 Yahweh willed it, and there was light.

6 Yahweh willed it, and life began.

7 Yahweh willed, and *all* creation was *very good.*[2]

8 As Yahweh wills, so it is.

9 The Divine placed Adam and Eve in the Garden of Eden and essentially said, "You are free. You are free to go everywhere and do everything. But some things can hurt you, and though you are free to do them, you should not. All things are lawful for you, but not all things will benefit your soul."[3]

10 God took his own breath and placed it into Adam and Eve.[4]

11 Yahweh takes His infinite freedom, the "I will be what I choose to be," and *breathes it into every one of us!*

12 The scriptures go so far as to say that we are called by Yahweh's Name.[5]

13 We are called by "I will be what I will be."

14 The essence of the Divine Name and nature, the liberty of free will, is the *heart and soul of who and what we are.*

15 You will be what you will to be; as Yahweh wills, and so it is, the same is true for you.

16 But do not be deceived. Jesus said, "The Kingdom of God is *within* you."[6]

---

[1] OT Exodus 3:14, FT Supplement 6
[2] OT Genesis 1:31
[3] OT Genesis 2:16 & 17, paraphrased
[4] OT Genesis 2:7
[5] OT Second Chronicles 7:14
[6] NT Luke 17:21

17 Your will controls your inner world: your thoughts, feelings, hopes and desires. That is where your will has absolute reign.

18 The outside world interacts with the will of everyone else.

19 To impose your personal will on everyone else would deprive *them* of *their* liberty.

20 God never deprives us of our liberty; we need to learn the lesson well.

Chapter 3
Evil Is the Cost of Liberty

1 Our notions about liberty are still too small.

2 Yahweh values freedom above and beyond all else.

3 The scriptures use the symbol of Adam and Eve being "free to eat from any tree in the garden"[1] to show they had liberty to experience everything the Universe has to offer.

4 Adam and Eve were even free to explore the tree that could hurt them: the Tree of Knowledge of Good and Evil.

5 Yahweh did not put this particular tree in the garden to "test" their obedience. This is a well-intended but misguided interpretation popular with the ways of old. Rather, God was warning Adam and Eve not to misuse their liberty.

6 The Tree of the Knowledge of Good and Evil could hurt them. Yahweh's admonition to avoid it was not a "test," but a *warning*.

7 We are free to go everywhere and do everything, even if it might hurt us. This was true for Adam and Eve, and it remains true for you.

8 God tried to warn Adam and Eve, but of course they would not listen. As above, so below: parents know all about childish rebelliousness.

9 They ate from the forbidden Tree, and thus were born ego, selfishness and separation. *Not* from disobedience, but because the Fruit of the Tree of Knowledge of Good and Evil *damaged them*.

10 The forbidden fruit "opened their eyes"[2] and changed their way of seeing the world.

11 No longer did they see with the simple eyes of childlike purity, knowing everything as it was: very good. But now they also saw *what was not*, and perceived this as lack.

---

[1] OT Genesis 2:16
[2] OT Genesis 3:7

12 Before the fall, they knew their naked bodies, and knew them to be very good. After the fall, they also knew they *did not have clothes*, and were ashamed. This was the birth of ego, selfishness and separation.

13 The story of the fall profoundly explains how all pain, suffering, theft, murder, greed, enmity and hatred resulted from Adam and Eve's *changed consciousness*.

14 Evil results directly from misuse of freedom.

15 God prefers the presence of evil to the elimination of freedom.

16 Yahweh could have limited Adam and Eve, making them unable to access the Tree of Knowledge of Good and Evil. But God Himself will not (*wills not to*) put a limit upon our freedom.

17 God would rather have evil in the world than a loss of freedom.

18 This is a lesson we must understand and take deeply to heart: God values liberty above all else.

19 Since God treasures freedom, so should we. As above, so below.

20 Freedom is the Heart of God, and liberty must be fundamental to who we are and all we do:

> We are free to explore, run, jump and climb.
> We are free to question, doubt, and learn.
> We are free to have fear and free to hope.
> We are free to love and free to hate.
> We are free to hurt; we are free to help.
> We are free to eat whatever we like.
> We are free to go where we will.
> We are free to do what we will.
> In the Divine mind
> we are, each of us,
> free without limitation.

21 But do not be deceived by your freedom: all things are lawful for you, but not all things benefit you.[1]

22 Not all things will help blossom your soul. Not all things will fulfill you.

23 Not all things will nourish the Fruit of the Spirit.

24 Not all things will help the Holy Spirit to come to fruition in your life.[2]

---

[1] NT First Corinthians 6:12
[2] FT Fulfillment 4:32 & 33

25 As Adam and Eve were warned to avoid what could hurt them, we are best served to heed the ways of wisdom, learning from others' pain,[1] that our freedom might be cause for celebration, not suffering.
26 You are free. But there are always ramifications to your freedom.

Chapter 4
Freedom Within

1 You embody the Divine Name, "I will be what I will to be."
2 Regardless of your external circumstances, you are free to perceive and react as you choose. Your soul will, indeed, be as you choose to be.

> You are free to love, and you are free to hate.
> You are free to hope, and you are free to fear.
> You are free to dream, and you are free to act.
> You might be rich but full of despair,
> or a pauper overjoyed with life.
> You can radiate vibrant health
> yet be sick of your very existence,
> or you may be seriously ill
> yet rejoice in the goodness of life.

3 As your spirit finds fulfillment, you will exercise self-control (an aspect of the fruit of the Spirit), recognizing that you *can* and *do* have ultimate dominion over all aspects of yourself.
4 As above, so below:

> You embody God's Name, "Yahweh,"
> meaning "I + Will = Being,"
> expressing liberty,
> which in your soul is absolute,
> which is perfect self-control,
> the fulfillment of the fruit of the Spirit.

---

[1] FT Pain 2:9 - 12

Chapter 5
Free from Attachments

1 Again, our notions about freedom are too small.

2 When we truly value the birthright of our divine liberty, we will never surrender it to *anyone* or *anything*.

3 You are free to think as you choose: social conformity is an insidious bondage to external control.

4 Freedom is more than self-indulgence: true freedom does not mean buying the latest apparel simply to be fashionable.

5 True freedom does not mean changing your hairstyle just to be stylish.

6 True freedom does not mean consuming music and food merely to gain social acceptability.

7 Fashion is slavery to an external force, no matter how good it might make you feel.

8 To be truly free on the inside *and* the outside is a concept that few are able to live.

9 We are subtly enslaved in many dimensions: politics, fashion, money, personal history, memory and religion.

10 We walk alike, we look alike, we act alike, we think alike and we talk alike. Millions of people buy the same exact product, deluded into thinking they are expressing their individuality.

11 Going to a job that provides no fulfillment, to get a paycheck that buys things which provide no benefit, is not freedom.

12 However, divine liberty does not mean abandoning our responsibility to our spouses and children.

13 Joyous fulfillment of responsibility is a clear expression of genuine freedom.

14 Narcissism is not liberty; it is attachment to selfish indulgence.

15 Why do we endlessly run around expressing our "freedom" by becoming ever more enslaved to the traditions, fashions and finances of the social order around us?

16 Do not be deceived: being in debt of any kind is slavery.

17 When you are in debt, part of your future is enslaved to paying for something that may well be gone or forgotten.

18 When you are in debt, you are in slavery. When you have financial debt of any kind, you *are* not and *cannot* be free. As the scriptures so wisely say, "Owe nothing to anyone except the debt of love."[1]

19 True freedom is much more than being able to choose the palace of your imprisonment.

20 Truth is the only religion.

21 And our notions about liberty are too small when it comes to religion.

22 Even well-intended parents destroy the liberated souls that God places within their children by expecting them to conform to traditional religious beliefs.

23 Most of us are raised to believe what we believe, simply because we are told to believe it.

24 The tiniest question or doubt can threaten us with a wide variety of punishments: loss of dinner, excommunication from church, risking our family's disappointment and, ultimately, total banishment from society.

25 Conformity is not freedom.

26 Embrace freedom from all "leaders" in politics, fashion, money and religion.

27 Challenge authority.

28 Think for yourself.

29 Moses was free to challenge the authority figures of his day, and this led to the Exodus.

30 An old man, Abraham was free to follow God's guidance, leave his homeland, and begin a grand adventure.

31 Jesus was free to stand up against the conventions of his day and challenge the religious leaders' proclamations.

32 The Future Testament encourages you to allow your children and yourselves the same freedom.

33 When we force our children into conformity, on any level, we are hindering their souls' growth.

34 Naturally, the younger the child, the more guidance is needed to avoid harm. But as the child grows, she must be encouraged to explore the world in all its aspects, to find out who he is really meant to be.

35 God encouraged Adam and Eve to explore all the world, with a loving warning along the way.

36 "Go and do likewise."[2]

---

[1] NT Romans 13:8
[2] NT Luke 10:37

37 Divine parenting invites children to express their natural freedom, even if that occasionally leads to harm.

38 Threatening children over religious issues denies their sacred liberty.

39 Always encourage questions, because they lead to knowledge.

40 God is never afraid of an honest question or a sincere doubt.

41 "Test Me, and see," says Yahweh.[1]

42 True liberty means that you are free to agree, *and* you are free to disagree. You are free to like, *and* you are free to dislike.

43 Liberty, at the Heart of God, is why the Future Testament can never be used as a form of coercion or a tool to force someone into submission.

44 That is the covenant you make if you resonate with the ideas of the Future Testament.[2]

45 You cannot force anyone else to like the Future Testament, and you must never coerce anyone into reading it. And certainly, you cannot ex-communicate your children if they do not find the Future Testament to resonate in their souls.

Chapter 6
The Natural Law

1 The sacred gift of divine freedom is the birthright of every human being.

2 As God breathed into Adam and Eve, as God breathed into Jesus, God has breathed into you.

3 Yahweh's Name lives in every single one of us. We all share the divine birthright of "I will be what I will be."

4 Divine freedom, the freedom that is absolute and unconditioned, exists *in* everyone and *for* everyone.

5 Therefore, you should not and *must not* use your freedom to interfere, limit or lessen the freedom of anyone else.

6 If you are to know the truth, and the truth is to set you free, then you must not use your freedom to diminish anyone else's liberty.

7 We must embrace each other's liberty as being as sacred as our own.

8 Divine Law is love, and the essence of that love is recognizing the oneness we have with God and each other.

9 The Law is Love.

---

[1] OT Malachi 3:10
[2] FT Covenant

10 This is the Natural Law: the expression of your divine liberty must never rob another of their divine liberty.

11 The only thing limiting your "limitless freedom" is everyone else's "limitless freedom."

> You are free, without limitation.
> So is everyone else. Therefore,
> you are free only insofar as your
> limitless freedom does not impinge
> on anyone else's limitless freedom.
> That is the only limitation.

12 But do not be deceived: you can use your freedom to harm others. We lie, we cheat, we steal, we abuse, we murder, we rape, and we invade other countries.

13 Violations of the Natural Law are called evil. Violations of the Natural Law are called sin.

14 The freedom that we hold so dear should never be used as a tool to rob someone else's freedom.

15 If we truly value *our* liberty, we will never deny another *their* liberty.

16 All social evils stem from denying another's liberty:

> Lying: in order to decide correctly, I
> need to know the truth. When you lie to
> me, you are denying my right to know.

> Stealing: when you steal something from
> me, you are denying my free use of my
> lawful property.

> Murder: you have denied
> me the liberty of life itself.

> Conformity: when you threaten me with
> ex-communication for not being
> politically correct, you damage the law
> of liberty that is supposed to ring through
> the world.

> Religion: when you threaten me if I do
> not agree with a particular religious idea,
> you are robbing me of Yahweh's eternal,
> infinite freedom.

17 The breath God first breathed into Adam and Eve, He breathes into all of us.

18 We are all tiny parts of God, made in His image, a miniature piece of the vast oneness of the Universe, given autonomy in ways that defy imagination.

19 We are individual drops of water which have bubbled off the face of the infinite ocean of God, every water drop containing all of the attributes of the ocean in miniature form.

20 Yes, you are free to abuse, to hate and to enslave. But those societies which have practiced genuine freedom for their citizens are those societies which have accomplished the most through history.

21 You are free to the fruits of your labors.

22 You are also free to give them away.

23 The danger of free societies has always been that the individuals become libertines, using their liberty to the point of excess, diminishment and loss, weakening themselves and their social order.

24 You will always remain free to hurt yourself and others.

25 But we can learn to use liberty for good.

26 Knowledge, truth and liberty: the three are one system.

27 The Future Testament is dedicated to those who work for freedom from slavery and external coercion, in every form.

28 Society will be free when all individuals are free.

29 We will all be truly free when the entire society is free.

30 Universal freedom is the pathway to infinite knowledge.

31 Free individuals create free societies, and free societies create free individuals. This, too, is a system.

Chapter 7
Proper Governance

1 If I use my freedom to harm you, I add to the hatred and violence in the world.

2 The extent to which I deny others their freedom is the extent to which I create a society birthing my own fear: fear of retribution and revenge, fear of uprising.

3 An environment of fear, oppression and violence cannot be truly free.

4 If you abuse others, you are creating the very environment that you seek to avert.

5 The tyranny, oppression and fear that we yearn to live without are created every time we use our liberty to harm others.

6 The only *proper* function of government is to deal with violations of the Natural Law:

> The expression of your divine liberty
> must never rob another
> of their divine liberty.

7 Dealing with violations of the Natural Law is why we need police and a military, for defensive purposes; *real* defense, not for unlimited aggression disguised with the word "defense."

8 We need government to oversee that businesses are operating freely and fairly. That is the proper function of regulation.

9 An autonomous judicial system assures that all violations of the Natural Law are dealt with fairly.

10 As the scripture says, better to have a millstone hung around your neck than to mislead one of Yahweh's children.[1]

11 We are *all* Yahweh's children. We are *all* born to live, to learn, to grow, to experience and to taste the fruit of every tree in the garden, even the ones that can hurt us.

12 The essence of evil is the loss of liberty.

13 If you are addicted to an external substance, you are not truly free.

14 If you are hurting another, you are not truly free.

15 If you are running from your responsibilities, you do not know divine liberty.

16 If you are using violence to seek your ends, you are not truly free.

17 A life that loves liberty will learn all truth and will value the freedom of all.

18 In your freedom, you have the divine opportunity to explore all knowledge, which leads us to The Book of Scripture.

---

[1] NT Matthew 18:6

The Future Testament

Book Three: The Book of Scripture

Chapter 1
The Closed Canon

1 Our ideas about scripture are too small.

2 Most use the word "scripture" to mean one specific set of writings, the only ones acceptable for religious guidance. The lists of holy books that are considered scripture vary greatly among traditions.

3 We are born into our native language, dress, morality, traditions and sacred books.

4 Society tells us that these special books are revealed and written by God, while the rest are the result of human effort or, worse, evil.

5 Alone among all books, the specific list of holy scriptures is said to contain spiritual truth. If another writing agrees with scripture, then it is redundant and unnecessary; if a writing says something different from the accepted scripture, then it is assumed to be evil, and therefore must be avoided. Our tradition may even *ban* such writings.

6 Only our sacred scriptures have value; all other writings are either excessive or wrong.

7 We are told our scripture is infallibly *revealed*; the rest are fallibly *reasoned*.

8 The Bible contains 39 books in the Old Testament. The New Testament has 27 books. These 66 books of the Bible have been voted by church leaders through history to be the scripture, a definitive collection of writings called the "canon."

9 Those who worship these books the most usually know the least about them. For many, they are the holy, inspired, perfect, inerrant Word of God. They are blissfully ignorant of the very fallible humans by which the Bible was written and the political processes that selected the authoritative canon.

10 Votes were taken, by men with political motives, to decide which books would be in the Bible. Women were not allowed a voice.

11 When anyone tells you what you can and cannot read, what you can and cannot study, what you can and cannot find inspirational, those people are limiting your freedom and robbing your divine birthright.

12 An organization that demands your allegiance to a particular book is trying to deprive you of your sacred liberty, beating your infinite God-breathed spirit into conformity with their limited view of the Universe.

13 In some groups, even reading a book outside the approved list risks criticism, or much worse.

14 Indeed, usually you are required to pledge your allegiance to their unique *interpretation* of chosen-by-vote sacred books.

15 The result is an infinite God limited by a finite collection of ancient texts, subjected to only *one* permitted interpretation, upon threat of banishment, excommunication or death.

16 This is not Yahweh's way. This is not Yahweh's wisdom of inclusion, freedom and love. This is not an expression of Yahweh's infinite liberty, your genuine birthright.

Chapter 2
The Open Canon

1 If your particular books, church and interpretation of truth are completely fulfilling to you, then the Future Testament is not for you.

2 You are free to ignore the Future Testament.

3 But please try not to despise those who are looking for something more.

4 The Future Testament invites you to expand your notions about scripture.

5 Do not say that you belong to a particular religion: all religions belong to you.

6 All religions are part of the history of the human race, which you inherited by birth.

7 All of history is a part of *your* story.

8 In this marvelous time, you have inherited the collective scriptures of Christianity, Judaism, Islam, Hinduism, Buddhism, Taoism and the other great faiths of the world.

9 If you can read this book, then when you were born, you received access to the sacred traditions of the entire world. Regardless of whether you received encouragement to explore them, all sacred scriptures of the world are part of your birthright.

10 In culturally divergent ways, all religions have expressed the Divine encounter with humanity: mankind reaching for God and God reaching for mankind.

11 All religions of the world do *not* say the same thing, nor are all religions the same. However, what they share is a heartfelt desire to comprehend God.

12 You are freely encouraged to learn from the scriptures of all religions.

13 Freedom is directly connected to scripture.

14 Knowledge and freedom are one system, a coordinated whole, each breeding the other.[1]

15 God has given you limitless liberty. Therefore you are free to examine the religions of the world. Anyone who would tell you otherwise is limiting God and trying to steal your birthright.

16 Say not that you hold fast to a single holy book; all books of every kind belong to *you.*

17 Say not that you belong to a specific cultural, racial or ethnic history; all of human history belongs to you.

18 Say not that you belong to a particular tradition; all traditions of the human race belong to you.

19 Say not that you belong to an exclusive group, for all groups belong to you.

20 No particular tradition, history, book, race, culture or church organization can have any claim on you. You belong only to God, and God gives you complete freedom.

21 The entirety of the human race is your birthright and inheritance.

22 Embrace the totality of all histories, people and religion with all that you are. Anything less is precisely what the Future Testament means when it says "your notion of scripture is too small."

23 You, Earth, history and God are one.

24 You are free to find holiness wherever you can.

25 You are free to find goodness, truth, inspiration and love wherever you recognize them.

26 You are free to find God-breathed wisdom wherever you realize it.

27 Allow no one to limit your limitless freedom to discover the fullness of God.

---

[1] FT Liberty 1:2 - 7

Chapter 3
The Fellowship of Religion

1 Part of the heritage of the Old Testament lies in the concept of Yahweh's people, the chosen ones.

2 The New Testament focused upon Yahweh's chosen *one*, his son Jesus, the anointed, the Christ.

3 And now, the Future Testament proclaims that *all* people are Yahweh's chosen ones.

4 *All* people are Yahweh's sons and Yahweh's daughters.

5 Jesus called us brothers, sisters and friends, equals to him.[1]

6 All religions can work together in harmony, free to disagree, but without anger, hatred or violence.

7 As we reach into the future there are some parts of our past that we must leave behind.

We must abandon the notion that
women are second-class citizens to men.
We must leave behind the idea that
slavery is in any way acceptable.

8 The extent to which these and other ideas were embraced by ancient people and their scriptures, must be recognized as cultural misunderstandings of the past, and nothing more.

9 We do ourselves and Yahweh a great disservice when we cling to evil in the ways of old, out of blind allegiance to a text.

10 If the book is found wanting, *any* book, then the book must be adjusted, and for that we need the discernment of the Holy Spirit.

11 Truth is the only religion.

12 We seek a Religion Beyond Belief.

13 We seek truth that transcends belief, fulfilled in knowledge.

14 We start with belief.

Belief that is *lived* becomes *faith*.
Faith that is *lived* becomes *knowledge*.

15 You will not find all religions to be of equal worth for you, nor will you find all books to be equally inspiring.

16 You are free to find truth wherever truth appears.

---

[1] NT Luke 6:40; John 15:15; John 20:17

17 If you are really searching for truth, it is silly to limit where you will look.

18 Pledge to leave no proverbial stone unturned in your quest for God.

19 Search the Law and the Prophets; search the Gospels and the Epistles; search the Koran; search the Rig Veda, the Upanishads and the Bhagavad-Gita; search the Lotus Sutras and the Tao Te Ching; search the world's philosophies, songs, paintings and poems.

20 You will find an entire world of people questing after God, and you will find evidence of Yahweh's constant quest to touch people's awakening hearts.

21 Your notion of scripture is too small if you are convinced that only *one* book written at *one* time with *one* frame of reference can be your eternal guide.

22 In the celestial banquet which is your destiny, and in the vast Garden of Eden which is your true home, you are invited by the Lord of Lords and the King of Kings, the God of time, space and dimension, to *eat from every tree.*[1]

23 Divinity's Children will feast upon the Tree of Life.

24 There is no reason to restrict your diet of wisdom and knowledge.

25 Open up to taste the many wonderful delicacies that fill the world.

26 You need not accept anything that a particular person or tradition teaches. They sought to grow and learn in their time, just as you are seeking to learn and grow in yours.

27 As a human moves from infancy into adulthood, so the human race is moving from infancy into maturity, full of love, wisdom and beauty.

---

[1] OT Genesis 2:16

Chapter 4
Sacredness

1 Our notion of scripture is too small when we make a distinction between the sacred and the so-called mundane.

2 We have misused scripture to divide our thinking between the "exalted" things of God and the "common" things of man.

3 We falsely separate our lives into the holy and the mundane.

4 Indeed, we ignorantly deceive ourselves by splitting the cosmos into divinity and humanity.

5 It was never meant to be so.

6 In the same way that we restrict our notions about scripture, we also limit our ideas of holiness.

7 All of life is an expression of Yahweh's Spirit poured into the Universe.

8 All truth expresses some aspect of the divine.[1]

9 Mathematical formulas are sacred Psalms.

10 A scientific understanding of the forces of the Universe is as blessed as the Gospel.

11 When we hear the voice of beauty speaking to us through music, that is the Voice of God.

12 We are one people, in a uni-verse, sharing experiences of truth, beauty and love.

13 As the scripture says, "There is no longer bond or free, male or female, Jew or Greek in Christ, but we are all one."[2]

14 The Future Testament invites you to erase the delusion separating the sacred and the mundane.

15 All truth is sacred. All truth is divine. All truth is a holy expression of our incomprehensibly glorious God.

16 The ineffable beauty of a dewdrop can make our hearts sing.

17 A math book can make us weep at the impossibly complex simplicity of the world.

18 The more we learn about blood cells, DNA, the structure of the eye and the mind-numbing glories of reproduction, the more we are learning about God and ourselves.

19 There is no barrier between the natural and the divine.

20 There are no boundaries between the sacred and the mundane.

---

[1] OT Psalm 19:1; NT Romans 1:20
[2] NT Galatians 3:28

21 Boundaries are illusions.

22 You are invited to find holiness everywhere, in everyone and everything.

23 Yet our notions about scripture are still too small.

24 The struggles of humanity recorded in history are holy scripture.

Biology books are scripture.
Chemistry, physics and astronomy books are all scripture.
Great literature, which teaches us about the human condition, is scripture.
Trigonometry, calculus, algebra, geometry…
all are sacred scriptures
written by the mind of God before time even existed.

25 Do not limit yourself by thinking that only the so-called holy books are scripture.

26 The Future Testament invites you to embrace the totality of all knowledge as your scripture.

27 Embracing all knowledge as scripture is the way we will heal the rift between science and religion, which has fractured our psyche for centuries.

28 Whatever the ultimate truth is, it must be cohesive, united.

29 The fundamental truths of religion *cannot* be different from the fundamental truths of science.

30 To know the unknown, to comprehend the incomprehensible, we must cultivate the mind of God.

If God caused the Universe, where did God come from?
No one knows.
What is this thing called life?
No one knows.
What is electromagnetism?
No one knows.
What is light?
What is gravity?
What is the unified field of which all physical energies are a part?
No one knows.

31 We can harness electricity but have no idea what electricity *is*.

32 We can smash the atom, but we have no concept of what an atom really *is*.

33 As we contemplate the deepest mysteries of existence, we can be
assured of several things:

The answers lie beyond the
limits of our weak, individual imaginations.
At every point in our history,
when we thought we knew everything there was to know,
we soon realized that we knew virtually nothing at all.
The answers must be unified.
Religious answers cannot be different from
scientific answers if both express truth.
Restricting ourselves to one particular way of
looking at the world, or a single tool by which we will
search for answers, unnecessarily limits us.

Chapter 5
Reason and Revelation

1 Some will say the distinction between scripture and non-scripture is
real, claiming that scripture contains God-ordained truth, whereas all
other books contain mere human understanding.

2 Scripture, they say, is divine revelation; all else is human reasoning.
Man reaches up; only scripture records God reaching *down.*

3 The Future Testament invites you to abandon these distinctions.

4 All ancient scriptures were written in a particular time and place,
within a specific worldview, expressed by a particular language.

5 Infinite Divinity, beyond space and time, must be expressed through a
particular language in a particular place and time, or nothing can be
said, and nothing can be known.

6 Limitless Yahweh, beyond time and space, is forever finding
expression within time and space.

7 All scriptures are shaped by the language and understanding of the
times they were written in because God could not convey concepts
without words, nor could people be asked to record ideas they
themselves could not understand.

8 Our knowledge has grown exponentially in 2,000 years. We can now
understand extraordinarily different parables than the very simple ones
Jesus taught.

9 Our comprehension has broadened so that now we can use the

parables of the automobile, the mainframe computer and the Mandelbrot set.[1]

10 All God-inspired writings are limited by the culture in which they were written, meaning they are prone to contain the misunderstandings of the prevailing culture.

11 The divine books of the Old and New Testaments (and, yes, they most certainly are divine) embrace slavery as being an acceptable form of living.

12 But now we realize that slavery is an abomination. At best, slavery was culturally acceptable in Biblical times, but slavery can no longer be tolerated. We are maturing, growing, learning more. It will forever be so.

13 We now recognize the higher divine truth: all persons are free, and all are born of the same God.

14 We see, then, that so-called infallible scripture is, of necessity, fallible.

15 God's revelation must pass through our reason in order to find expression.

16 As God and man are one, as the sacred and mundane are one, so too revelation and reason are one.

17 As knowledge and liberty are one system, so too are revelation and reason.

18 All reasoning is an outpouring of divine revelation. Our ability to think is none other than the divine mind placed in us.

19 All revelation is married to our reason.

20 God's ability to reveal infinite truth is none other than our ability to comprehend rationally.

---

[1] FT God Chapter 3

Chapter 6
Trinity: The Three Are One

1 The Future Testament invites you to go beyond the distinctions of human writing (reason) versus divine writing (revelation).

2 In days of old, God was thought to be "out there," a white-bearded gent sitting on a throne in the great beyond, with an infinite gulf between Himself and humanity.

3 In the ways of old, God was wholly other, completely separate from us.

4 The Future Testament invites you to embrace a more comprehensive vision.

5 Through our scientific investigations, we now know that nothing is ever created or destroyed. The conservation laws reveal that things only change from one form into another. The famous equation $e = mc^2$ means that energy (e) and mass (m) are different parts of the same system.

6 Celebrate unity beyond the appearance of diversity:

Science reveals that energy and mass are
twin aspects of a unified essence.
Male and female are different states
of a fundamental, underlying reality.
Water, ice and steam are
different *versions* of one element.
In exactly the same way,
the sacred and mundane are approaches
to a unified underlying essence.
Reason and revelation are different
approaches to the same knowledge.
Divinity and humanity are as coupled
as electricity and magnetism.
The Future Testament invites you
to cease thinking of God as
being separate from you.

God is not so far away that He cannot be found:
God is so close that He is overlooked.
God is both what you hear
and the power by which you listen.
God is both what you see
and the power by which you look.
God is both what you know
and the very ability to know.
God is both who and what you love,
and the power by which you love.

7 As adding heat changes H_2O from ice to water to steam, so too "the renewing of your mind"[1] changes the mundane into the sacred.

8 As energy and mass can change states from one to the other, so too God can be transformed into humanity and back again.

9 This is not pantheism.

10 The totality of God lies far beyond the boundaries of our imaginations.

11 To equate God with nature, with matter alone, energy alone, or the totality of all energy *and* matter, is a mistake.

12 The material Universe is God's physical body.

13 We are each a holon of God, a small part of the limitless whole.

14 We are made up of *nothing except God!*

15 The scripture says, "in God we live and move and exist."[2]

16 You live in God. You move around in God. You exist inside God.

17 A blood cell floating in your bloodstream does not belong to anyone but you. It is a part of you, and in its own partial way, the blood cell *is* you.

18 In exactly the same way, you are made up of *nothing but God.*

19 Learn the parable of the blood cell: God is to you as you are to your blood cell.

20 As the distinctions between you and God blur and fade over time, the Future Testament invites you to a new way of understanding knowledge.

21 Every single time you "know" something, God is *what* you know *and* the power by which you know it, for God is the totality.

22 Every time humanity discovers a new scientific truth, that discovery is a thought in the mind of God as received through a human mind.

---

[1] NT Romans 12:2
[2] NT Acts 17:27 & 28

23 Into each moment of comprehension God breathes life, the very consciousness He originally breathed into Adam and Eve.

24 The Future Testament offers that, whenever *anyone* discovers *anything*, a part of Yahweh's mind is *in* the individual, *doing* the discovering. God is the only reality, there is nothing else.

25 God is also *what is being discovered*. God is the only reality, there is nothing else.

26 God is actually rediscovering the glory of God.

27 God is the only reality; there is nothing else.

28 The Bible even tells us this: only God's mind can know the thoughts of God, and we have the mind of Christ.[1]

29 When you know something, you are the part of God that knows it.

30 This is the mystery of the Trinity.

31 Some object to the idea of the Trinity, but it is actually infinite truth in embryo. Consider:

> The Father and the Son are *one* in the Spirit.
> The giver and receiver are *one* in the gift.
> The lover and the beloved are *one* in love.
> The speaker and the listener are *one* in speech.
> The transmitter and the receiver are *one* in the signal.
> Subject and object are *one* in relationship:
> the three are *one*, a trinity.
> The subject-object-relationship is one *system.*
> All trinities are one system. The three are *one.*
> As God is everywhere and everything,
> and God is a trinity,
> it is only reasonable to find
> triune relationships to be
> the essence of all existence, everywhere.
> You and the Father are one,
> in the very same Spirit
> breathed into Adam,
> and incarnated as Jesus.

32 For the Future Testament, there is no distinction between reason and revelation.

33 All discoveries of pure reason are a revelation of God, and all of Yahweh's revelations merge with our human reason.

---

[1] NT First Corinthians 2:11 & 16

34 Reason and revelation are one in knowledge: the Trinity in conscious expression.

35 The separation between *divine* truth and *human* truth must become a part of the past, the same way notions about slavery and female subservience must disappear.

36 Transcend the illusion of sacred and mundane.

37 All knowledge is God-breathed.

38 All knowledge is scripture.

39 The Future Testament invites you to explore all realms of knowledge with an enhanced appreciation of both reason and revelation.

40 This is the way to heal the schism between science and religion.

41 We will find that truth really is united; that science and religion are different aspects of the same truth, just as energy and mass are reflections of each other.

42 Sacred and mundane, male and female, God and humanity, knowledge and freedom, reason and revelation, science and religion; all are one system, existing as paired opposites, expressing the transcendent underlying Reality.

43 We will know that the Universe was not created in six days, or even 14 billion years.

44 We will know that the Universe has not evolved by random chance or selective mutation.

45 We will learn that all life and truth are being developed by a Transcendent Intelligence that goes far beyond our current imagination.

46 When you recognize the so-called opposites as equal partners, you begin to live a fully God-breathed life.

Chapter 7
Scripture Equals Knowledge

1 Scripture equals knowledge.

2 Everything that can be known is scriptural, and everything that can be discovered is sacred.

3 Ancient man lived in a world where everything was animated with divine mystery and excitement, and yet he was ignorant.

4 Modern humanity has been learning the incredible depth, complexity and vastness of the Universe, yet we have lost our wonder.

5 The Future Testament invites you to a renewed experience of excitement, exuberance and zest for life, reveling in the wonders that our reason and rational intelligence have brought to us.

6 Thousands of years ago, the Sun was a magical object, worshiped by early humanity. The Sun should be even more wondrous for *us*, now that we have learned so much about how vast and complex it really is.

7 If the ancient people could have reverence for the Earth and every living thing, how much more so should we?

8 If early mankind could revere the rocks on the ground, how much more so should we?

9 What if the rock were to tell its full story, or the rock bed, or the volcano, or the ocean, or the Earth herself?

10 What if Jesus' statement, "…the stones will cry out"[1] became literally true? Such knowledge cannot yet be borne by the human mind.

11 The Future Testament invites you to see every mathematical formula as a joyous dance of the Divine and the chemical tables as the glorious spice cabinet Yahweh has used to develop the Universe.

12 The Future Testament invites you to open your mind *and* your heart; do not rely on one or the other, but connect the sweetness of heart with the rationality of mind.

13 Let your mind *and* your heart fall in love again, like an old married couple who fell out of love due to a misunderstanding, only to rediscover their love, precisely *because* of all the time they spent apart.

Divinity's Children,
approach every moment,
each experience
and all knowledge
with the same joyous exaltation
found in your highest,
holiest sacred experiences.

14 All life is scripture.

15 All knowledge is scripture.

16 Liberty is the pathway to knowledge, the fulfillment of your life.

---

[1] NT Luke 19:40

Chapter 8
A Trinity of Knowledge

1 Knowledge exists as a trinity: what is *true*, what is *right* and what is *good*:

> True (false): The realm of "it"—objective reality, fact, science
> Right (wrong): The realm of "us"—society, convention, morality
> Good (bad): The realm of "me"—personal opinion, preference, art

2 That which is *true* is immutable, external and perfect. That which is *true* is objectively scientific: the speed of light, the force of gravity, the identities of mathematics. These are unchangeable truths which stand *apart* from humanity.

3 That which is *right* is the realm of social convention. It is *right* (righteous) to be honest. It is *right* to not murder. It is *right* to be a kind and loving person.

4 The Future Testament says it is both right and righteous to embrace all knowledge as sacred. The realm of rightness lies in-between what is *true* and what is *good*: our culture calls it morality, the intersection of humans with each other.

5 That which is *good* is the realm of opinion. Your favorite music is *good*; your preferred cuisine is *good*; the movie was *good*. These are personal preferences.

6 *True* ("it"), *right* ("us") and *good* ("me"). The three are one, like ice, water and steam.

7 Many of our problems come from regularly mistaking one for the other, confusing fact for convention, confusing morality with art.

8 A person of power can declare his *good* to be socially *right*, and therefore objective *truth,* for all people everywhere.

9 Thus are born fascism and tyranny of all kinds.

10 Preference and opinion are functions of the mind and heart and are constantly changing. What one says is *right* may not feel *good* to you; what is *good* to you may be objectively *wrong* to someone else.

11 Parents deal with *right* and *good* on a daily basis. As children grow and mature, behavior that is *right* or *good* for a toddler is unacceptable in a teenager.

12 Similarly, something that was *right* in the Bible, like slavery, we now recognize as neither *right* nor *good*.

13 The Old Testament says God commanded Joshua to slay his enemies,[1] and this perceived *truth* was *right* and *good.*

14 However, in the New Testament, Jesus commands that we love our enemies and pray for them![2]

15 Our understandings of scientific *truth,* social *right* and personal *good* change drastically over time.

16 Our notions of truth, righteousness and goodness constitute the essence of conflict when it comes to scriptural fundamentalism.

17 Religions of every kind confuse divine *truth* with cultural opinions of *right* and *good.*

18 A personal preference (*good*) quickly becomes the enforced expectation of the group (*right*) and ultimately the proclamation of ecclesiastical *truth.*

19 As you grow in knowledge, the Future Testament implores you to be discerning, separating immutable *truths* from the conventions of *rightness* and opinions of *goodness.*

20 When you can properly differentiate between what is true, right and good, then you can embrace all truth, righteousness and goodness, as *your* scripture.

May you have the
discernment to tell the
true from the right and the good,
as your **Liberty**
finds **Fulfillment**
in the **Scriptural**
system of triune knowledge,
encouraged to
grow through **Faith**.

---

[1] OT Joshua 6:21 & 10:40
[2] NT Matthew 5:44

The Future Testament

Book Four: The Book of Faith

Chapter 1
Religion Beyond Belief

1 Our ideas about faith are too small.

2 What passes for religious faith today is of little worth.

3 Faith has fallen from its lofty role as a divine gift into the pits of doctrinal argument.

4 Today, when people speak of "faith," they usually mean belief in ancient dogmas and creeds.

5 So-called saving faith is little more than *belief*: giving agreement, often coerced (physically, emotionally or financially), to ancient religious ideas. These ideas cannot be proven and seldom touch the essence of your life's destiny.

6 Church "confessions of faith" are long litanies of religious doctrines, hammered out hundreds of years ago, mainly as *political compromises* among disputing factions.

7 Denominations tell you that if you do not believe their creeds, then you do not have "faith" and are therefore displeasing to God.

8 But in our modern world, there are millions of people who are not inspired by ancient dogmas.

9 The Apostles', Nicene and Athanasian Creeds are recited weekly. But for many spiritual seekers, the words of these doctrines reflect a time long past and contribute *little* to the challenges of today's world.

10 For many, the creeds offer nothing to have faith *in* and are of no help living today's reality.

11 Belief, no matter how sincere, does not constitute *faith*.

12 Real faith involves your *life*.

13 Something may speak to you. You may even believe it. But you demonstrate genuine *faith* when you begin to *live your life* by it.

14 The Future Testament invites you to a radical change:

Religion Beyond Belief.

15 Religion Beyond Belief means two things:

16 First, the essence of religion lies far beyond the realm of simple belief.

17 The word "religion" comes from the Greek *re* (again) + *ligare* (bind, connect).

18 Therefore, in its roots, "religion" means to *re-connect*, to *rejoin*.

19 To be religious means to re-connect with the experience of God-breathed life.

20 "Religion Beyond Belief" means that the real spiritual life is much more than believing in creeds.

21 Second, "Religion Beyond Belief" means that the real life of the Spirit, faith and oneness with God, goes *beyond* the bounds of current imagination.

22 Real religion goes beyond what we can currently believe.

23 If you could catch a glimpse of your fulfilled, perfected life, you just "wouldn't believe it!"

24 You are invited to experience *Religion Beyond Belief.*

Chapter 2
From Belief to Faith to Certainty

1 Real faith is a living power. As the scripture says, "Faith is the assurance of things hoped for, the conviction of things not seen," and "faith without works is dead."[1]

2 You may *believe* that the moon is made of green cheese. But you have *faith* the person driving behind you has brakes that work. You are literally putting your life on the line for the latter, and the former simply does not matter.

3 Your *life* matters. Faith that *touches* your life also matters; belief that does *not* touch your life is immaterial.

4 You are free to believe in anything you wish because God created you to be free.

5 *Belief* cannot change your life, but when you live your life *according* to your belief, then belief becomes a living *faith.*

6 Belief is an opinion, an assumption, a guess.

7 You are best served to have as few beliefs as possible.

8 An excess of pointless beliefs, unconnected to any testable, present reality, clogs the mind and dilutes the soul.

---

[1] NT Hebrews 11:1; James 2:26

9 Everyone has faith.

The question is: what do you place your faith *in*?

10 Nations, religions and individuals argue, hate and go to war over beliefs about what may (or may not) have happened two or three thousand years ago.

11 Abandoning ancient and needless beliefs, *we will be free!*

12 The Future Testament invites you to renounce beliefs of the *past* that do not serve the *present*.

13 People most violently defend that which they least understand and have the least confidence in.

14 When you actually *know* something, you have no reason to hate another who doubts.

15 Only those things we secretly doubt can generate angry responses.

16 No one has ever killed another for not being able to understand the Pythagorean Theorem!

17 Beliefs, unconnected to living faith, of *necessity* lead to violence when given soul-saving authority by external churches.

18 As you enter the realm of Religion Beyond Belief, you will experience an increased presence of God in your daily life.

19 As you experience God and *know* the truth beyond belief, you are set free.

20 You will be free from the need to prove the rightness of your beliefs or lash out against someone who might not believe as you do.

21 The Future Testament has no desire to give you a new set of beliefs to replace your old ones. That accomplishes nothing.

22 Just as real morality is more than swapping one set of vices for another, real religion is more than exchanging one set of beliefs for another.

23 The Future Testament offers a different way of approaching religion and life: beliefs become faith that can be lived, examined and tested, leading to certainty of knowledge.

24 "Test me,"[1] Yahweh says.

25 As Saint Paul said, "Now abide three, faith, hope and love; but the greatest of these is love."[2]

26 Love is the greatest because love *knows*.

---

[1] OT Malachi 3:10; NT First John 4:1
[2] NT First Corinthians 13:13

27 Notice the essential connections: freedom breeds knowledge; knowledge can be contained in scripture; scripture can lead you to a living faith that takes you to the same certainty of knowledge Jesus demonstrated.

28 Watch for these connections as the twelve-pointed star of the Future Testament unfolds.

29 How do we know *what* to have faith *in*?

30 Many say that *all* religion is false. How can we know?

31 Since faith is "the assurance of things hoped for, the conviction of things not seen,"[1] how do we decide where to place our faith?

32 How do we separate truth from falsehood?

33 How will we determine the criteria by which we answer Pontius Pilate's profound question to Jesus: "What is truth?"[2]

34 Which holy book or religious authority should we trust? And how do we know if our teacher is telling the truth?

35 Feelings, thoughts, visions, dreams, clergy, books, sermons and media: all can help, but all can mislead. How are we to proceed?

36 Truth is the only religion.

37 Transcending belief with faith, and transcending faith with certain knowledge, what criteria do we use to determine truth?

38 Simply put, the Future Testament invites you to apply the scientific method to your spiritual life.

Chapter 3
The Scientific Method

1 The Future Testament is working toward the glorious reunion of the twin sisters of human consciousness, religion and science.

2 Their reunion will provide a wondrous gift to the religious life: the scientific method.

3 The scientific method is perhaps the greatest accomplishment in the history of the human race.

4 The scientific method approaches knowledge *systematically*, beginning with a question. "Why do birds fly?" or "Why is the sky blue?" or "Why is diamond harder than cobalt?"

5 The scientist then reads the research of those who have come before him or her in their examination of the question.

---

[1] NT Hebrews 11:1
[2] NT John 18:38

6 The magnificent gift of literacy must be considered the birthright of every human being on Earth.

7 In order to learn something, you can either learn it yourself or, if you are literate, you can learn it from someone else.

8 We learn most quickly with access to the wise life efforts of those who have come before us.

9 Having done the research, the scientist then forms his or her best answer to the question. This educated guess is called the "hypothesis."

10 The scientist then *tests* the hypothesis by performing experiments, gathering data and evaluating the hypothesis in light of the data.

11 Scientists then publish their results to the world so that those who come after them can benefit from their efforts.

12 And you inherit it *all!* It is all your *birthright!*

13 Every experiment, thought, result and book in the history of humanity belongs to you, so that you might see the ever-widening vistas of infinity that comprise our Universe.

14 The Future Testament invites you to apply the scientific method to your own religious life.

15 In your quest for spiritual truth, the scientific method is the best model for answering Pontius Pilate's question.

16 Begin with a question. Is there life after death? What is justice? Are miracles real?

17 The real passion of scientists is found in their burning questions. They *need* to know.

18 What question is burning in *your* heart? Explore it.

19 How is it that anything exists? Why are we here? Who am I? Who are we? Where did God come from? What is God's name?

20 What do we mean when we propose applying the scientific method to religion? We simply follow the same steps scientists do, except we are exploring the realm of the spirit.

21 Having formulated your question, you are then free to examine the world's scriptures.

22 What answers have the saints of old found? What does the literature say?

23 Having read the research, proceed to the third step of your investigation: create your hypothesis.

24 Untested hypothesis is belief.

25 Untested hypotheses are meaningless. To be valid, a hypothesis must be testable, tested and explored.

26 Religious hypotheses must be *lived.*

27 In religion, the hypothesis phase is a test of the "assurance of things hoped for and the conviction of things not seen."

28 Faith is a lived (tested) religious hypothesis.

29 Faith is not an end in itself, but a means to an end.

30 Belief is only a starting point.

31 Belief is fulfilled in faith, faith is fulfilled in knowledge, and knowledge is fulfilled in love.

32 By living our lives, we test the scriptures to see if they are true.

33 We test the Word of God. We test our faith, and if our faith holds true, it becomes our knowledge.

34 Having performed your living experiment, examine the data. What did you hear? What did you feel? What did you see?

35 Was there a measurable outcome of your experiments?

36 Did you see God? Did you hear His voice? Were you listening? Were your experiments valid? Did you experience the power of forgiveness? Did you find hope fulfilled in the knowledge of love?

37 As you examine the data, remember: "In the beginning was the Word."[1] "Word" comes from the Greek *logos*, meaning logic, reason and language.

38 So our religious conclusions will be logical and reasonable.

39 For example, if God as parent is a sound model of divinity, then certain conclusions about the nature of God can be logically deduced.

40 With the results of your research and experimentation, re-examine your faith.

41 When you have come to your conclusions, publish them.

42 How you "publish" those results is the life you live. Perhaps you write a book, create art, write a song or volunteer at a food kitchen.

43 Your life is the 151st Psalm. You are the fifth Gospel.

44 The scientific method is a profoundly effective way of gaining knowledge, with broad application to religious life.

45 Though they have spirited debates, scientists do not have to argue about facts. The goal of science is to go beyond debate, belief and hypothesis into the realm of knowledge.

46 Either an experiment's result is verifiable or it isn't.

47 The Future Testament shares the goal of knowledge.

48 You shall *know* the truth, and only knowable truth will set you free.

49 What you believe is at best a starting point, becoming faith only as you apply your life to it.

---

[1] NT John 1:1

50 Yahweh's Love is the oneness that encompasses all thoughts, feelings, emotions, desires and bodies.

51 The fulfillment of His Love is Yahweh's destiny for you.

52 God does not require allegiance to belief. He doesn't ask that you argue with other people about *their* belief systems, trying to justify a belief system which you can neither understand nor explain.

53 The scientific method, applied to your religious life, can set you free from the tyranny of ancient creeds.

54 Welcome to the world of the Future Testament.

55 Welcome to Religion Beyond Belief.

Chapter 4
Touching Life

1 As you apply the scientific method to your living faith, you will discover thoughts, beliefs and ideas that need to be discarded.

2 Like panning for gold, the dirt and pebbles of Earth's past are washed away to reveal the shining nuggets of eternity.

3 Like tuning the radio, you have to filter out the background noise to be able to receive the signal.

4 The process of living faith requires clearing the cobwebs and discarding the junk from the musty attic of old belief systems.

5 You will need to wash away ideas of male superiority and female subordination.

6 You will have to turn off the noise of slavery and prejudice of every kind.

7 You will need to abandon all notions of someone else doing anything vicariously for you.

8 The journey toward infinite truth and God consciousness is long, and you must travel lightly.

9 Fighting to hold onto archaic doctrines will prevent progress.

10 Only hold to what matters here and now.[1]

11 There is no need to erase the histories of humankind and our colorful stories of the past. They will inform you and confirm your own development. But you do not need to hold onto myths of the past as though they are literally true.

12 Stories need not be historical fact in order to contain truth.

---

[1] NT Matthew 6:34

13 If you are holding onto the beliefs that God physically talked through a donkey[1] or stopped the Sun in the sky for two days,[2] you will have difficulty moving ahead.

14 The life you live matters. People matter. Hold to what is important, and do not carry excess baggage.

15 Perhaps an ancient story actually occurred, or maybe it was total fabrication. Neither will actually touch your life.

16 Never take a living position on what does not touch life.

17 The stories of the past can be guides and hints, but only that.

18 Doctrines of the church that cannot be tested and do not affect your life are of little worth.

19 When you have *experienced* death and resurrection, you need not argue about Jesus' bodily resurrection—you *know* resurrection to be a fact.

20 When you have visions that become reality, you will no longer need to dispute another's vision.

21 When you have experienced healing, you need not worry about the historicity of Jesus' miracles.

22 When you have seen and participated in miracles, you no longer require ancient texts to confirm your reality.

23 The stories of the Bible are here to inspire hope, to arouse dreams and to build faith that grows into experience and knowledge.

24 Scripture seeks to transcend all need for scripture. Scripture seeks to lead you into direct experience.

25 In the past, ecclesiastical structures decided which writings become scripture.

26 Here in the Future Testament, everything is different.

27 Only *you* can determine if the Future Testament is scripture for you.

28 Your life matters. Allow no ecclesiastical structure or government to decide for you.

29 The unexamined, externally coerced belief system is not worth having. You are worth much more than a forgery passing as spirituality.

30 The true purpose of scripture, the real purpose of the Old, New and Future Testaments, is to lead you to the reality they point to and thereby *become unnecessary*.

---

[1] OT Numbers 22:28 - 30
[2] OT Joshua 10: 12 - 14

31 Like an able teacher, all scripture seeks to become irrelevant, having fulfilled the purpose of teaching: to connect the student to the direct experience of what is taught.

32 Once you understand the essence of Euclid's Elements, you no longer need the math book.

33 Once you have lived a life of resurrection, the Bible is unnecessary.

34 This is not to say that you will *abandon* your scriptures: the roots of your tree of life are vital to the growth of the entire tree and the fruition of your soul.

35 Like the tree, in order to grow and bear fruit, your soul must reach up. But living exclusively for the roots leads to burial, darkness and death.

36 At the same time, the tree without roots is likewise dead.

37 The New Testament makes it clear that unless Jesus' death and resurrection become your own, then Jesus' death and resurrection are of no use to you.[1]

38 In this way, the Future Testament is leading back to the very heart of the Bible.

39 Jesus pointed to a living faith, a physical embodiment of the religious life.

40 Saint Paul understood, and followed his lead.[2]

41 Neither Jesus nor Paul wanted their words and experiences turned into doctrines for us to fight about.

42 Rigid religious doctrine sends the world to hell in a basket woven of ideas created thousands of years ago—ideas we no longer understand and cannot support, which do not touch life. And yet we *kill each other* over these ideas!

43 Jesus wept.[3]

44 The Future Testament invites you to apply the scientific method to your life.

45 Transform your beliefs into a living faith hypothesis, and test that hypothesis with your body, soul and spirit.

46 You will come to a *direct* understanding of yourself, your fellow human beings and the God of the Universe.

47 Your understanding will transcend all writings, creeds, doctrines and beliefs.

---

[1] NT Romans 6:3 - 5
[2] NT First Corinthians 11:1; Galatians 2:20
[3] NT John 11:35

48 You will come to certain knowledge, and the knowledge will be love.

Chapter 5
The Power of Faith

1 Our notions about the power of faith are too small.

2 Jesus spoke of the living power of faith, saying, "If you have faith like a mustard seed, you would say to this mountain 'be gone' and it would be gone."[1]

3 Jesus could have said, "If you have faith like a mustard seed, you could say to this light beam 'heal this blind eye,' and the eye would be healed."

4 Jesus could have said, "If you have faith like a mustard seed, point sound waves at the belly of a pregnant woman and you will see her unborn baby."

5 Gigantic earth-moving machines *do* move mountains.

6 The foreman of the job says, "move that mountain," and the mountain is gone.

7 Miracles need not be flashy, supernatural events.

8 Faith is not just the content of ancient books and miracles.

9 When humanity gets over its petty squabbles and sectarian differences, we will accomplish the miraculous, far beyond even our current phenomenal world.

10 No one human can build a skyscraper; no one human can build a computer; no one human can land on the moon.

11 But by *cooperating*, we have been able to populate the planet with skyscrapers and build computers that communicate with each other, and humanity has indeed walked on the moon.

12 With the tiniest mustard seed of faith, we can do all of these wonders and so much more.

13 The Future Testament herein states unconditionally and without reservation:

Every single problem in existence can be solved.

14 Poverty, starvation and disease can be eliminated.

15 All war, injustice, crime and fear can be eliminated, if we have the faith of a mustard seed to work together as one race.

---

[1] NT Matthew 17:20

16 More connections: you need *freedom* to be able to gain a *faith* which we can test to turn into certain *knowledge.*

17 Through *knowledge* we gain *power.*

18 Through the knowledge of how light works, laser beams were developed for "miraculous" eye surgeries.

19 Through the understanding of how sound works, we developed devices that echo ultrasound waves into a woman's womb to see her growing fetus, without harming woman or child.

20 Daily, we read our email and drive our cars and fly our airplanes, all of which would have been beyond miraculous to ancient man.

21 As we live in the consciousness described in the Future Testament, we will be living faith, bound together as one people.

22 The wisdom of our re-connected hearts and minds will enable us to perform miracles, the likes of which we cannot imagine.

23 Religion Beyond Belief.

> In faith-filled love we will
> say to cancer *be gone,*
> and it will be gone.
> In faith-filled love we will
> say to poverty *be gone,*
> and it will be gone.
> In faith-filled love we will
> say to disease *be gone,*
> and it will be gone.
> In faith-filled love we will
> say to scarcity *be gone,*
> and it will be gone.
> In faith-filled love we will
> say to hatred *be gone,*
> and find it already gone.
> In faith-filled love we will
> say to suffering *be gone,*
> and it will be gone.
> In faith-filled love we will
> find the fruit of the Spirit filling all people.
>
> With living faith,
> we pray in Your holy and Infinite Name,
> Amen.

The Future Testament

Book Five: The Book of the Law

Chapter 1
Misunderstanding the Law

1 Our notions about law are too small.

2 To address the concept of law in the Future Testament may appear to be a contradiction to some. If we are eternally free and limited only by the Natural Law,[1] then it may not be apparent why we need law at all.

3 For centuries, Christian theology has considered the Law "a curse." The New Testament refers to Christ as "having saved us from the curse of the Law."[2]

4 The Future Testament refers to misunderstandings in classical Christian theology as "the ways of old."

5 The ways of old tragically distinguish between Law and Gospel.

6 According to the ways of old, the purpose of Law was to reveal our sin and to convict us of it, so that we might be able to accept redemption as a gift of grace through Christ.

7 The same theology said that the Law was a slave master: to violate one command just *one* time would be the same as violating *all* the laws *all* the time.

8 The Torah defines 613 laws: 365 things you must *not* do and 248 things you *must* do.

9 The thinking went like this: one violation of Yahweh's Law would result in eternal wrath, for Yahweh's justice could not tolerate the presence of sin.

10 Such ideas are not Yahweh's truth. They are a part of the cultural misunderstandings of the past which must be transcended. These ideas fail when the scientific method is applied. Philosophically, rationally, sociologically, such ideas make God into a monster.

11 The good news of the Gospel can only thrive in harmony and love with the Law.

12 There are different ways the word "law" is used.

---

[1] FT Liberty 6:11
[2] NT Galatians 3:13

13 Today, "following the law" refers to human laws, which are nothing more than the rules we use to play this game called society.

14 Speed limits and tax rates change like the weather. These are not true laws; these are rules—fickle, arbitrary and often silly rules established by human beings to manipulate the social order.

15 The precepts God gave to Moses in Torah became the Old Testament laws: hundreds of commandments as to what we *should* do and hundreds more as to what we should *not* do.

16 For the early Jews, attempting to live according to every single one of the laws of Moses may indeed have felt like a curse.

17 It was nearly impossible to live perfectly following the major ten commandments. However, many of the Mosaic "laws" were actually cultural rules given for the protection of Yahweh's people, such as dietary rules to ensure health and counteract disease.

18 This does not make them wrong nor trivialize the Hebrew Law.

19 But what is right at one time in one place is not necessarily true at all times and all places.

20 The challenge of examining sacred texts is to discern eternal truths from cultural traditions.

21 As we saw in the Book of Liberty, God gave Adam and Eve full freedom to explore the Garden and to do anything and everything they chose to do.

22 The Future Testament then discussed the Natural Law: you are free to do whatsoever you choose, so long as your freedom does not impinge upon another's freedom to do what they choose.

23 We saw how the Natural Law is connected to the Great Law (or moral law): "You shall love the Lord your God with all your heart, with all your soul, with all your mind and with all your strength; and you shall love your neighbor as yourself."[1]

24 The Great Law is a deepening, a maturation of our understanding of the Natural Law.

---

[1] NT Matthew 22:36 - 40

25 The term "law" also refers to the nature of the Universe:

the law of gravity,
the law of electromagnetism,
the law of force equals mass times acceleration,
the law for every action there
is an equal but opposite reaction.

26 In order for the world to enter the next stage of cooperative Religion Beyond Belief, the Future Testament invites you to a new vision, celebrating the glories of law.

27 The Law is not a curse, and it never was. This misunderstanding must be set aside.

Chapter 2
The Law Is Love

1 The Future Testament does not wish to replace one set of beliefs with another.

2 You are encouraged to examine, test and decide for yourself.

3 Our hypothesis: God is *at least* as loving as a human parent. If the hypothesis is true, what would religion look like, based on this understanding?

4 In the Book of Faith, the Future Testament talks about the joys of using the scientific method as an approach to your life and religion.

5 This idea will no doubt infuriate many.

6 The scientific community thinks religion has no value; therefore applying the scientific method to religion is a meaningless exercise.

7 Much of the religious community will consider such an approach blasphemy.

8 If you are resonant with the text of the Future Testament, you will understand the need to harmonize our spirits with law in the same way we need to reunite religion and science.

9 The truly religious life need not be afraid of science and its discoveries.

10 Truth is one.

11 Truth is the only religion.

12 There can be no disagreement between the truth of real science and the life of real faith.

13 Instead of animosity, the Future Testament invites you to celebrate each mathematical and scientific law as a new discovery about the Creator.

14 The true life of Spirit need not to be anxious about Yahweh's Law as though it is some kind of curse.

15 Rather, real Law is cause for celebration and rejoicing.

16 What ultimate tragedy to think of divine Law as a curse, because God the Father is Love.

17 Jesus tries to make this crystal clear: the greatest law is to love. Love God; love each other.

18 The Law is Love!

19 Love is the Law!

20 Since Law equals Love, it *cannot be a curse!*

21 God only wants what is good: your fulfillment.

22 If you really want to understand law, understand parenting.

23 A loving parent "lays down the law" with her children from the time they are babies. This law serves only one purpose: love.

24 True law seeks to serve, protect, and keep from harm.

25 True law is love.

26 Good parents never create laws to *test* their children's obedience.

27 Let's return to the beginning. The ways of old thought the forbidden fruit was Yahweh's test of Adam and Eve's obedience. But it was never so: Yahweh did not try to *test* Adam and Eve, but *warn them*. The purpose of the story is to illustrate how the fruit of the Tree of Knowledge of Good and Evil could hurt them. This is a profoundly deep matter.

28 A loving parent does not create arbitrary tests, nor conceive of "eternal punishment" when the children fail those tests.

29 A loving parent could never use law as a method to keep track of wrongs in order to calculate a punishment. This is another misunderstanding of the ways of old.

30 Parental laws *protect* and *warn*.

31 Parental law is *love*.

32 Moms and dads "lay down the law" in order to protect their children and keep them out of danger.

33 In order to help children avoid hurt and pain, the loving parent gently disciplines.

34 Real discipline is not judgment or recompense, but *teaching*.

35 Test this, and examine it, and live it in the core of your being:

> Real, loving discipline gives a
> small hurt children *can* understand,
> in order to avoid far greater
> pain children *cannot* understand.
> The notion of "eternal punishment"

is, by very definition of the words,
inconceivable for a loving parent.

36 The laws of good parents try to prevent the child's unintended,
self-inflicted harm.

37 When you love your children, there is no parental law they could
break that would make you disown them; it is beyond imagination.

38 There is no guidance your children can ignore that could cause
you to curse them forever.

39 Certainly, there is no law that is more important than your
children and no mistake they could ever make that would cause you to
condemn them forever.

40 *It is impossible for you to love your children more than Yahweh
loves you.*

41 Old interpretations tell us that if we disobey just one law, just
one time, "God" will cast us into the eternal flames of hell.

42 To the ways of old, one little violation of the Law gets you
God's punishment for all eternity.

43 The "God" of the ways of old is a psychotic parent, despotic and
evil.

44 Be not deceived: the ways of old ascribe psychopathic behavior
to our Heavenly Father: delivering laws only as arbitrary tests,
monitoring obedience for its own sake and punishing eternally.

45 Test, examine and live this deeply:

Justice has no meaning as a thing in itself!
To speak of God as having two natures,
love and justice, is an error.
Justice only has significance as it serves love.
Justice is never an end in itself,
only a means to an end.

46 God is Love.[1] True love always gives guidance and direction.

47 The good parent sets limits on her child because the younger the
child, the more incapable she is of understanding the hurt she can do to
herself with her liberty.

48 As the child grows, she will internalize an ever-growing
understanding of the limits of liberty, and the dangerous pitfalls of
human life.

---

[1] NT First John 4:8

49 As she matures, she will grow to internalize the moral system and the proper use of her liberty on her path to fruition.

50 In exactly the same way, the human race as a whole is like a child growing up.

51 In Old Testament days, God had to guide humanity with a system of absolute laws where personal freedoms were rare. Yahweh was guiding infant humanity, as a parent protects a newborn.

52 God started with iron-clad laws that seem to soften in the New Testament, as Jesus talks of love and forgiveness.

53 But be not deceived: the laws of the Old Testament and the love and forgiveness of the New Testament *are not separate.*

54 The Law and Love are one, just as religion and science are one, just as God and humanity are one.

55 The Law and the Gospel are one.

56 The revelation of Yahweh's moral law in the Old Testament was wonderful guidance:

> "Hear, O Israel, and be careful to
> obey so that it may go well with you
> and that you may increase greatly
> in a land flowing with milk and honey,
> just as Yahweh, the God of your fathers,
> promised you."[1]

57 Human misunderstandings turned the Law into a curse.

58 Dietary laws for desert-wandering nomads were interpreted as eternal truth, even after the Jews became farmers and city dwellers.

59 We anoint our cultural traditions as eternal truths.

60 Similarly, human misunderstanding made us believe that to violate one precept of law would forever curse us from the Heart of God.

61 It was never true. Ever.

62 Test this, and examine it, and live it in the core of your being.

---

[1] OT Deuteronomy 6:3

Chapter 3
Law Is Harmony

1 In Old Testament days, God in His wisdom commanded the wandering Jews to avoid shellfish and pork. In the Sinai desert, eating shellfish or pork could put your entire family at risk.

2 Yahweh's command was not a restriction. It was not an arbitrary test: it was blessed guidance to prevent illness and death!

3 The overwhelming majority of the laws in the Torah are *blessings*, guidance and loving direction.

4 Our bodies are systems, and they work according to laws.

5 The same electro-mechanical laws that govern spaceships, cars and computers also affect our bodies, only in different ways.

6 Just as the Christ descended into space and time to become Jesus, Yahweh's holy breath enters into space and time to become all of us.

7 We live in the realm of matter, of physics, chemistry and biology.

8 Knowledge of the realm in which we live gives us power: power to live according to the truths of Law.

9 The truths of physics, chemistry and biology are nothing more or less than the laws of the Universe.

10 You cannot fall off the Earth. If you eat poison you will die. If you poison your soul, you will be damaged. If we hurt one another we create a world of pain.

11 Here is the glory and the beauty of true law: true law is utterly dependable, not like smaller human rules we call our "law."

12 The laws of the Universe are absolute and immutable:

Electromagnetism

Gravity

The strong and weak nuclear forces

For every action there is an equal but opposite reaction

Force equals mass times acceleration

13 The greater our understanding of the laws of the Universe, the more we can work in harmony with them.

14 The laws of the Universe were created to be the womb of our soul, not as some curse.

15 We can place our faith in the universal laws because the universal laws do not change. They are absolute and immutable.

16 The universal laws become the foundation upon which we build the Kingdom of God.

17 Our souls also work according to law.

18 The more we love Yahweh's moral law, the laws of the Universe and the Natural Law, the more we will bring the laws of society into harmony.

19 The more closely our lives reflect Divine Law, the more harmonious our lives will be.

20 The more closely our social rules reflect Divine Law, the more harmonious our planet will be.

21 The Future Testament recognizes the futuristic nature of these ideas.

22 Imagine the world perfectly in harmony with Yahweh's moral law, the laws of the Universe and the Natural Law.

23 "Faith is the assurance of things hoped for, the conviction of things not seen."[1]

24 Imagine our world transformed: all of humanity rejoicing in their liberty and acknowledging the liberty of all other beings, with the Natural Law as the basis for all social law.

25 Imagine all human beings faithfully exploring Yahweh's laws of the Universe as clues to the unfolding glories of the invisible Spirit, growing and reveling in absolute knowledge. This is the world, fulfilled.

26 That is the hope of the Future Testament; that is the heart's desire of the people who wrote this book.

27 That is our prayer, and the vision for which we work.

28 It is the promised destiny of the human race, as Divinity's Children begin to awake.

---

[1] NT Hebrews 11:1

Chapter 4
Science and Religion

1 When the Psalms were written, the rift between science and religion did not yet exist.

2 The early psalmist, in reverent appreciation for the natural world's power and beauty, wrote, "The heavens declare the glory of God and the Earth shows His handiwork."[1]

3 The psalmist knew that everything around us could teach us something about God.

4 Reverence for nature continued into the New Testament. Saint Paul tells us, "Since the creation of the world God's invisible qualities—his eternal power and divine nature—have been clearly seen, being understood from what has been made."[2]

5 The material Universe is a window into the heart of the Divine.

6 We cannot encounter each other's souls directly.

7 Your mind has to express itself through words, gestures and body language; your feelings and emotions are expressed through the body.

8 Every moment of every day, we are expressing the immaterial (that which is within us) through the material (our bodies).

9 The material Universe is a window into the mind of the Divine.

10 Through the material world, we endeavor to catch glimpses of the immaterial spiritual realities that lie beyond.

11 This is one of the oldest ideas: "As below, so above."

12 In the Torah, we learn how Moses was shown the tabernacle he was to fashion as God's dwelling place on the Earth.

13 We do "down here" what we first imagine "above."

Every skyscraper started with an idea.
Every symphony started with a hope.
Every painting started with a dream.
Everything in this physical world started as a thought.

14 This is one of the great debates that will be resolved over the next several hundred years.

15 One of the great issues we will eventually resolve is the nature of consciousness itself.

---

[1] OT Psalm 19:1
[2] NT Romans 1:20

16 Either consciousness proceeds from matter (electrons and protons combining to generate consciousness), or vice versa. This is known as the great mind-brain debate.

17 The Future Testament invites you to test the notion that this world proceeds from a spiritual transcendence that utterly defies our minds.

18 Many scientists are beginning to agree with this position.

19 On the cutting edge of quantum mechanics and nuclear physics, many say that matter ultimately *acts like consciousness*.

20 We are also discovering that every physical reality appears to have a spiritual parallel:

> The law of physics states that
> for every action there is an equal
> but opposite reaction;
> the Law of God says that
> "As you give, so shall you receive."[1]
> As the densest matter is
> connected to pure energy,
> the highest spirit touches
> the lowest matter.

21 Science and religion have much to learn from each other.

22 As energy and mass are a continuum ($e = mc^2$), so too are spiritual and physical law.

23 The Law of God and the Laws of Nature are reflections of each other, parallels in the domains of spirit and matter.

24 The Future Testament invites humanity to turn its social rules into Laws that reflect the harmony of spirit and matter.

25 As above, so below.

26 The spirit–matter relationship is so profound that we will spend the rest of time exploring the glorious parallels.

---

[1] NT Matthew 7:12; Luke 6:31

Chapter 5
Connect to the Earth

1 The true spiritual life consists of divine *and* physical Law, and letting them both be the model for moral law.

2 When you can read a math book and weep at the intricate beauty of the Universe, you are in the Heart of God.

3 When you can find the glories of chemistry uniting with the laws of electromagnetism to create physics, you are beginning to understand the truth of God.

4 The Future Testament invites you to love, serve, re-serve and con-serve our glorious Earth.

5 The ways of old said we needed to *subdue* the Earth. The Future Testament invites you to test, examine and live the wisdom of *befriending* the Earth.

6 It is insanity to pretend that you love God so much that you need pay no attention to any part of His glorious Universe.

7 Knowledge is power, and knowledge of our physical world has enabled human beings to live longer, live healthier and have the opportunity for true spiritual fulfillment.

8 This is a sacred trust.

9 The ways of old abuse humanity, claiming that only its creeds matter to your eternal soul.

10 But be not deceived: growing into knowledge can also hurt. This is part of the message we should have learned from the story of Eden.

11 As liberty can be used to harm others, knowledge can kill.

The power to light a bulb
gives the power to electrocute.
The power to keep warm by the fire
confers the power to burn people alive.
Knowing how to kill harmful bacteria
confers the power to create biological warfare.
Comprehending the structure of the atom
enables us to perform nuclear medicine
and destroy millions of innocent people
with the push of a button.

12 This paradox is why science and religion *must* remarry.

13 This is why Christianity must learn to fall in love with Law.

14 Unless our moral development keeps pace with technological advances, we will remain on the verge of annihilation.

15 A hundred years ago, it would have been unimaginable for a child to carry a gun into school; now it happens daily.

16 What begins as a thought becomes an experiment (like Edison's light bulb) and soon becomes a worldwide phenomenon.

17 Now people can turn on a light without needing to touch a switch.

18 What begins in one imagination quickly becomes available to all.

19 Technology becomes ubiquitous.

20 If technology continues to run rampant because spiritual people deny all responsibility, caring only for ancient creeds, then humanity has lost its soul.

21 If the devout lovers of God simply wait for Jesus to snatch them off the Earth, so they don't have to deal with any of the problems we face, then humanity is lost.

22 The Future Testament *begs* the human race to remarry its two great rivers, science and religion.

23 We need to re-sacralize science by finding ecstasy in every scientific and mathematical truth.

24 We need to experience Law as grace and beauty, as Yahweh's outpouring of Divine Love.

25 We cannot leave the ability to manipulate matter unchecked, lest society become a soulless zombie.

26 Science and religion truly are one, waiting for us to rise above our petty differences.

27 Truth is the only religion.

28 Embrace the Natural Law *and* the laws of physics. Make them the basis of social law.

29 The true, the right, and the good: correctly differentiated *and* working together.

30 God and people, one. All people, one.

31 Liberty and knowledge, one.

32 Religion and science, one.

33 As you love law, you will discover the eternal truth of the Gospel: not Law *versus* Gospel, but Law *and* Gospel.

34 Law and Gospel, one.

The Future Testament

Book Six: The Book of the Gospel

Chapter 1
The Crux of the Matter

1 The Cross is the crux of the matter.

2 The Cross is the crossroads, where everything connects:

> The Cross is the connection of time and space.
> The Cross is the connection of inside and outside.
> The Cross is the connection of time and eternity.
> The Cross is the connection of God and humanity.
> The Cross is the connection of above and below.
> The Cross is the connection of everything you are
> and everything you will ever be.

3 Our notions about the Cross are too small.

4 A new understanding of the Gospel is essential to the fulfillment and continuation of life on Earth.

5 Thus far, the Future Testament has offered a glimpse of the fruition of your soul, your genuine freedom, the marriage of knowledge and revelation and the celebration of the truth of scripture wherever such truth is found.

6 Now we come to the heart of the matter, the center of the Christian message.

7 The Cross is the heart of the matter.

Chapter 2
The Euangeleon

1 In order to reclaim what the Gospel should mean, we have to understand what the word "gospel" originally meant.

2 The English word "gospel" derives from the Greek word *euangeleon*:

eu- meaning "good"

and

- *angeleon* meaning "message"

3 The euangeleon was a messenger sent by the Greek army to proclaim victory to the people.

4 When Greek armies were fighting a war in a distant land, the people of the cities not only lived in fear for their beloved sons, but also lived in support of the armies; they were living on rationed food, textiles, horses and metals.

5 Once victory was achieved, it was the role of the *euangeleon* to ride with "swiftness of foot" (sometimes his own literal feet) to proclaim victory as quickly as possible.

6 The restrictions of rationing would be over, and the people could rejoice in the "good message."

7 The idea of the euangeleon is a magnificent illustration for what the Gospel was intended to be for every one of us.

8 We all need to hear the good message that all enemies are vanquished and victory is ours.

9 Christ was victorious over the enemies of sin and death.

10 Though he died, he was resurrected.

11 "It is finished,"[1] he cried.

12 Just like the euangeleon, what remained was for someone to carry the good message, the good news, to the people.

13 For this, the Gospel exists.

14 It is up to each one of us to accept the message.

15 Once we accept the message of the *euangeleon*, the previous victory becomes our present reality.

---

[1] NT John 19:30

16 This is the heart and soul of Jesus' proclamation, "Behold: repent, for the Kingdom of Heaven is at hand."[1]

17 The word "repent" means to go beyond your current thinking, to look at yourself and your life differently.

18 Repentance means to change your mind.

19 Transform your thinking, because war is over!

20 Sin and death are vanquished. The Kingdom of Heaven, where Divinity reigns absolutely, is at hand. It is here and now.

21 All we have to do is change our thinking from being caught inside the life of "rationing," that dreary, sinful, war-like ego state, to the promised life of love, joy and peace: the fruition of the Spirit, the life of fulfillment.

22 The Gospel is about the transformation of your life, about turning away from darkness and selfishness into the present reality: the victory of Yahweh's Kingdom.

23 The Gospel offers the gift of infinite love, joy and peace, which is our genuine birthright as we accept the good message for our lives.

Chapter 3
The Good News of Responsibility

1 The Gospel comes with social responsibility: feed the hungry, aid the poor, clothe those who are naked, visit the sick and comfort the widows.[2]

2 Your personal salvation becomes social salvation as you turn from your selfish ways to embrace the Kingdom of God, helping all those around you.

3 We move from self-centered to global-centered consciousness. "Thy will be done"[3] means to align ourselves with Yahweh's will.

4 This turning, this repentance, was meant to be the event that ushered in the Kingdom of God, the second coming of Christ.

5 We were meant to be free from the past, to celebrate the joys of the victorious present and eternal future.

6 But something happened along the way. We got lost. We took a detour.

---

[1] NT Matthew 4:17
[2] NT Matthew 25:31 - 46
[3] NT Luke 22:42

7 Personal transformation requires inner reflection and deep private involvement.

8 Personal transformation calls us to social action.

9 Over the course of time, the Gospel message began to change.

10 In the Sermon on the Mount, Jesus said, "Therefore, you are to be perfect as your Father in Heaven is perfect."[1]

11 The root word translated "perfect" is also where we get our word "telescope." The telescope allows us to see something far away, bringing it close, and making it larger to our eyes.

12 That's how Yahweh sees perfection.

13 Though it is small, a sapling is a perfect tree.

14 Though she is young, a kitten is a perfect cat.

15 Likewise, Yahweh looks at us through the telescope of time, seeing us fulfilled.

16 Simply because we have much to learn does *not* mean we are imperfect.

17 For Jesus, the *only* measure of our perfection is love.

18 If you love your enemies, you are perfect.

19 The only requirement is love; all else is commentary.

20 But Christians started to think that being perfect was just too difficult for them: "Certainly Jesus did not really mean what He said in the Sermon on the Mount, did He? I mean, no one can be perfect."

21 They wanted to maintain their normal, selfish, sinful ways yet be assured of going to the heavenly place when they died.

22 Through the centuries, the church has been very eager to cater to this selfishness and, in so doing, maintain power over the people.

23 The Gospel of transformation became diluted with political creeds, and the universal cult of belief was born. The Gospel became an abstract belief system.

24 Jesus' life, death and resurrection were no longer guidelines for taking up your *own* cross[2] and following his path. They became a mythology that no longer required any involvement on your part, as long as you *believed* that Christ took up his cross *for* you.

25 According to the cult of belief, you don't have to go through your own personal ego-death, as long as you believe that Jesus did it *for* you.

26 The cult of belief says that you do not need to tread your own pathway to Golgotha, just so long as you are willing to watch Jesus

---

[1] NT Matthew 5:48
[2] NT Luke 9:23

walk it *for* you. You don't have to rise to newness of life, effected by your own repentance, as long as you believe that Jesus rose from the dead *for* you.

27 Belief became a substitute for spiritual rebirth.

28 This is the most grievous error taught by the ways of old.

29 These erroneous attitudes have given rise to the notions of vicarious atonement ("vicarious" meaning experienced through another as a substitute), vicarious salvation and, ultimately, vicarious life.

30 Confessing doctrines became a substitute for the dedicated spiritual life Jesus modeled.

31 As long as you recited the confessions, you were free to get on with the rest of your life exactly as you were before. Continue tithing, and you would receive the weekly pronouncement of forgiveness.

32 For centuries, even to this day, uncountable millions of "Christians" have found their highest form of communion with God to be forgiveness. Forgiven of every sin they ever committed, past, present and future, free to go out and do them all again, because they will, indeed, be forgiven again next Sunday.

33 By the millions, "Christians" confess on Sundays that they did horrible things during the week, but because they believe Jesus paid the penalty for their sins, they feel free to continue their wicked ways.

34 Listen to the conversations in almost any fellowship hall, on almost any Sunday, in almost any country, and you will hear this attitude expressed in countless ways.

35 By contrast, *real* personal transformation, to truly be "born again," is a continual process that Saint Paul illustrated when he said "Behold brothers, I die daily."[1]

36 Genuine spirituality involves time, effort, commitment and concentration.

37 Jesus weeps.[2]

---

[1] NT First Corinthians 15:31
[2] NT John 11:35

Chapter 4
Forgiven Christians

1 Since the cult of belief's notion of salvation is vicarious, its religious life is also vicarious. Thus, the real life in the Spirit stays one step removed from us.

2 Jesus, it is said, communes with God so we don't have to.

3 Diluted Christianity is left with a 21st-century bumper sticker attitude which says, "Christians aren't perfect, just forgiven."

4 Boiled down to its essence, this attitude means a Christian is not to be trusted to tell the truth, to be fair with you in business, to be alone with your spouse, or to watch your children, any more than their secular counterparts are.

5 The cult of belief's essential doctrine is that, when the Christian confesses the magic creed, God no longer holds their wickedness against them. In every other way, the Christian remains identical to their unsaved neighbor.

6 Their confession becomes their truth. 21st-century "Christians" are virtually indistinguishable from those outside the church.

7 Numerous sociological studies have shown that divorce, alcoholism, drug use, narcissism, greed, selfishness, debt, spousal abuse, child abuse and violence are virtually *identical* inside and outside the church.

8 To people with ravaged lives, the church has become unable to offer much more than platitudes and positive thinking.

9 When a young person from a Christian home gets into trouble with crime, alcohol or drugs, or goes to jail or rehabilitation, the church has little to offer: no purpose for life, no notion of the growth of the Spirit, no sense of fulfillment, nothing.

10 All too often, the only vision a young person is offered is a sad life of work, consumerism, debt and forgiveness—the "opportunity" to become the same empty member of society they see around them.

11 "Without a vision, the people perish."[1]

12 In far too many Christian churches, the sense of living, sanctifying growth in the Spirit is absent. The opportunity to become a light-being of infinite love and joy is neither offered nor modeled.

13 The transforming fire of the Spirit has all but been extinguished.

---

[1] OT Proverbs 29:8, King James version

14 For all intents and purposes, in far too many Christian churches, the Gospel is dead.

15 It was never meant to be this way. Jesus did not want it this way. It need not remain this way.

16 The Future Testament has not come to abolish the Gospel, but to fulfill it.

Chapter 5
Everything Old Is New Again

1 Our notions about the Gospel are too small.

2 Today, the word "Gospel" means many different things to millions of different people.

> For Catholics, "Gospel" means being
> adopted into the One True Church.
> For Mormons, it means being baptized
> into the "only true and living
> church upon the face of the whole earth."[1]
> For Lutherans, it means giving
> assent to the Augsburg confessions.
> For New Age churches, it means
> ceasing to think negative thoughts so that
> you attract only goodness to your life.

3 All of these notions are too small.

4 The Gospel of Jesus Christ is not some theological proclamation that we agree with in order to be free to pursue our normal lives.

5 The Gospel is not a set of ideas with which you must agree in order to be "saved."

6 The Gospel is not a long recitation of the nature of the holy Trinity you must believe (even if you don't understand) in order to be "saved."

7 Jesus made it plain that he had one desire for us. He prayed the burning desire of his heart in his high priestly prayer, "That all of them may be one, Father, just as you are in me and I am in you."[2]

8 And yet, Christian denominations war against other Christian denominations. Churches fight, bicker, splinter and sue one another in court. Why is this? How can this possibly be?

---

[1] Doctrine and Covenants, 1:30
[2] NT John 17:21

9 Churches have taken their eyes off the true Gospel, turning it into meaningless small-minded arguments about creeds and doctrinal purity.

10 These notions about the Gospel are far, far too small. As a result, Christianity is dying a slow death.

11 We need the Future Testament because the world around us is changing so quickly. Our wonderful world is becoming one, whether Christianity is ready for it or not.

12 At the turn of the 21st century, the individual countries of the European Union began to behave more like states than countries. Such unions are proliferating, because there are many advantages to union over separation.

13 The hallmark of the second Christian millennium was *competition*; the hallmark of the third will be *cooperation*.

14 The day *will* come when we see the "United States of the World." This is a necessary part of the growth of the human race.

15 Some will see this as evil because they're afraid of the future. But humanity *is* one, and *will* express that oneness.

16 Over time, humanity is growing from:

egocentric
(I, me and mine)
to ethnocentric
(identifying with one's race)
to nationalism
(patriotism, country-consciousness)
to globalism
(world citizenship).

17 If the human race survives, we might even make it to intergalactic citizenship!

18 All of this begins with the notion of you, who you are and what you identify with.

19 Who are "you"?

Are you only the individual?
Do you care only for your family?
Do you identify with your race?
Is your essence one particular geographical location?
Or do you identify with the entire human species,
with all creatures and with the Earth herself?

20 Both the Bible and the Future Testament invite us to a world-centric view:

21 "In Christ there is neither Jew nor Greek, there is neither slave nor free man, there is neither male nor female; for you are all one in Christ Jesus."[1]

22 We are all one family under God.

23 And yet, 2,000 years later, Christianity seems *less* prepared and *less* inclined to live this promise because of small-mindedness.

24 Christians focus on meaningless doctrinal issues that divide, and ignore the living Gospel that would unite.

25 Small-mindedness identifies Christianity with creeds, escalating into bloody wars lasting centuries.

26 Devoid of its true heart, Christianity is dying. Membership is down across generations, most nations and traditional denominations.

27 As a force for social change, Christianity is virtually impotent.

28 The death of Christ's message has led to a new style of church, working to feed the narcissistic I/me/mine civilization bred by rampant consumerism.

29 Meanwhile, the heart of Christ still calls us to genuine resurrection.

Chapter 6
Resacralization

1 The Future Testament seeks not to *abolish* the Gospel, but to *fulfill* it.

2 Let the theologians and denominations argue.

3 The Future Testament will celebrate the good news that Jesus came to proclaim, that John the Baptist, Saint Paul, Saint Peter and so many others came to proclaim, good news the world so desperately needs to hear now.

4 Hear it again, as though for the first time:

Change your thinking!
The good news is that God is at hand!
God is here! God is now!

5 Embrace this one idea, absorb it and live it. It will lead you to a kingdom of joy unimaginable.

---

[1] NT Galatians 3:28

6 God is at hand. "Jesus came proclaiming the Gospel, saying the time is fulfilled and the Kingdom of God is at hand. Repent [change your thinking] and believe in the Gospel."[1]

7 Most of us sadly shuffle through life, going through the motions without any knowledge of *who* we are, *where* we are, *why* we are or where we're *going*.

8 But Jesus said to repent—he said we need to change our way of thinking. Why? Because God is here! The Kingdom of God is at hand!

9 *This* is the eternal truth of the Bible we need to take *literally*.

10 The Future Testament is here to help you re-sacralize your life, to help you find the sacred joy in even the smallest of things:

> Cooking dinner for the family and
> eating together is not a burden;
> it is an incredible joy.
> Finding labor that you
> delight in is a blessing.
> Sleeping through the night in
> safety is an incredible gift.
> Having sanitation facilities is a
> sacrament denied to far too many people.
> Clean water, fresh air,
> food, friends, family,
> the glories of nature,
> music, art, sacred texts,
> consciousness itself...
> God is here! God is now!

11 "And God saw all that He had made, and behold, it was *very good*."[2]

12 That's the *real* good news, the genuine Gospel.

13 Change your thinking, because God is here!

14 Changing your thinking isn't a one-time event, but a life-long process.

15 Like Paul, we must die daily to the small self and embrace Yahweh's will for our lives.

16 Jesus admonished us not to worry about what we eat, drink or wear.[1]

---

[1] NT Mark 1:14 & 15
[2] OT Genesis 1:31

17 He spoke of taking no thought for tomorrow, because each day has enough troubles of its own.[2]

18 The only thing worth paying attention to is what Jesus called the "pearl of great price,"[3] God's presence.

19 The Kingdom of God is in your midst. The Kingdom of God is in you.

20 Saint Paul talked about the "mystery of the ages"[4] that has been hidden in plain sight all the time, and is indeed the good message.

21 This "mystery" is the greatest gift, best secret and supreme joy of all time: that Christ is *in* you, and desires to live *through* you, *as* you.

22 Becoming Christ is a lifelong experience.

23 To use classical language, the process of sanctification by which we are made holy goes on forever.

24 This, and only this, is the real Gospel.

25 Our notions about the Gospel are far too small.

26 In its fullness, salvation means to make whole, to "salve" or heal all the wounds of ego, pride, selfishness, greed, resentment and sin. In that healing, we are made whole and holy.

27 When our eyes and ears are opened to the truth, when we have eyes that see and ears that hear, then we recognize that, indeed, God is here.

28 Our waking consciousness becomes one in which we die to the old ways and are resurrected to the new ways of Christ-being, every hour of every day.

29 Make no mistake: every day there will be trouble remembering that becoming Christ is the only struggle worth having.

30 Belief is a necessary step along the pathway, but it is never an end in itself.

31 Confessing our sins and being forgiven are means to an end, never an end in themselves.

32 Belief, confession, forgiveness, communion: all are means to the heart-felt, mind-felt, open-armed *experience* that God is here.

33 This is the real good news, the true Gospel.

34 You are *already* forgiven. Yahweh's forgiveness for you is infinite; the forgiveness of a Heavenly Father and Heavenly Mother.

---

[1] NT Matthew 6:31
[2] NT Matthew 6:34
[3] NT Matthew 13:45 & 46
[4] NT Colossians 1:25 - 27

35 Remember the euangeleon: the victory has already been accomplished. All you need to do is realize it.

36 Quite possibly, the Jewish people's greatest contribution to the history of human ideas is the notion of God as parent. If you are a good and healthy parent, you know there is nothing your child could do that would make you stop loving and forgiving her.

37 Is God a bad, petty parent?

38 Let the theologians argue about vicarious atonement, doctrines and dogma—these don't matter.

39 What matters is that Yahweh's forgiveness is eternal, infinite and absolute. We simply need to repent (change our thinking) in order to tap into Yahweh's forgiveness.

40 Much like the electricity that runs through our walls, we must "plug in" to experience forgiveness.

41 There are no magic formulas or secret rites needed for God to find us worthy of forgiveness.

42 The euangeleon has already declared victory. We are already forgiven. Each of us must *realize* the forgiveness that is already ours.

43 When we accept the good news of the Gospel-euangeleon, the previous victory (Jesus' experience) becomes our present reality. Yahweh's eternal forgiveness becomes our present reality here and now, as we repent and receive His forgiveness.

44 Still, forgiveness is simply a means to an end.

45 What really matters is that we learn to love.

46 Being forgiven is meaningless if we do not forgive.

47 Being loved is meaningless if we do not love.

48 Eternal life begins now.

49 Having eternal life is meaningless if we are not fully alive; that's why we are denied access to the Tree of Life until we are fully alive.

Chapter 7
Life Matters

1 The life you lead matters.

2 Jesus' immortal words in the Sermon on the Mount ask us to forgive, to love, to be merciful, to pray for our enemies and to bless those who persecute us.

3 Theologians destroy the true power, glory and promise of the Gospel when they tell us Jesus didn't care about how we live.

4 What you do with your life matters. All of Jesus' parables tell us this.

What you do with your money *matters.*
Helping those less fortunate *matters.*
Being compassionate *matters.*
Forgiving your enemies *matters.*

5 Confessing creeds does not save you.
6 Doctrinal purity does not matter.
7 Christ in us, living as God in the flesh... *matters!*
8 The real Gospel is a perfect, crystalline whole:

You are free to do whatsoever you desire.
Your freedom is best used as an
expression of love to help others
find their love, joy and goodness.
Yahweh's forgiveness is eternal.
The life you live in freedom matters.
You are invited to find
scripture everywhere because
God is here, and God is now.
Change your thinking;
go beyond your current way
of looking at the world.
Go beyond your current
understanding of religion.
Go beyond your current
understanding of Gospel.
Law and Gospel are one.
Go beyond your current ways
of understanding God.
The Kingdom of heaven is in our midst.
It is right here; it is right now.
The life you live matters;
Christ *will* be formed in you.
Living the Gospel,
Divinity's Children will feast upon the Tree of Life.

The Future Testament

Book Seven: The Book of Christ

Chapter 1
The Real Christ

1 Our thoughts about Christ are too small.

2 We speak of the body of Christ but have little idea what we are talking about.

3 We talk about the mind of Christ or the heart of Christ yet have a very small grasp of their meanings.

4 We use the words "Spirit of Christ" but, like words flashing on a screen, we hear the words without a depth of understanding.

5 The Future Testament offers a fervent prayer that we re-connect to the original meanings of the body, mind, heart and spirit of the Christ, as revealed in the New Testament.

6 Far too few even know what the word "Christ" really means.

7 Sadly, many millions of people actually think that Jesus' last name was "Christ."

8 The English word "christ" derives from the Greek word "christos," which comes from the Hebrew word "messiah."

9 "Messiah" means the anointing of God. King David of the Old Testament had the anointing of God. Many of the Old Testament prophets were said to have the anointing of God.

10 Originally, "messiah" meant the oil used for anointing, and later, the special blessings conferred by that anointing.

11 To use our modern term, King David, the Old Testament prophets and Jesus were "Christ-ed."

12 To be "Christ-ed" means to be anointed or blessed and ordained. The words are directly related.

13 Over the course of time, "the anointing" has come to refer to only one person in history: Jesus of Nazareth, born of Mary.

14 The crucial Gospel message, that we are *all* supposed to be anointed by God, has been reduced to *one* person, *one* place and *one* time: Jesus of Nazareth, in Judea, the year 30 A.D.

15 It was not supposed to be this way.

16 The anointing of God was placed upon Jesus the man.

17 Jesus' anointing was dramatic and mesmerizing to behold: upon Jesus' baptism by John in the Jordan River, the Holy Spirit descended like a dove and God spoke, "This is my son, in whom I am well pleased."[1]

18 What everyone must know, what the church must return to, and what the Future Testament seeks to restore, is the intimate understanding that everyone, *every single person on the Earth*, is supposed to have this anointing.

19 Every single person is supposed to become Christ, the anointed of God.

Chapter 2
Subject or Object?

1 When Jesus walked the Earth, he demonstrated that he was a religious subject to be *followed.* He said so repeatedly:

2 "Come, *follow* me," Jesus said, "and I will make you fishers of men."[2]

3 "Then Jesus said to his disciples, 'If anyone would come after me, he must deny himself and take up his cross and *follow* me.'"[3]

4 He was a guide for us to *follow.*

5 Jesus' life journey is meant to model our pathway to Christhood.

6 Jesus is a religious subject to imitate.

7 As Saint Paul said, "Imitate me, as I imitate Christ."[4]

8 All the things that Jesus did, we are meant to experience ourselves, in our own way, in our own time.

9 We are meant to find the anointing of God on us.

10 Like Jesus, we are meant to be declared the Christ.

11 Yahweh intends us to heal, to cast out demons and even to resurrect others from the dead.

12 Since each of us is unique, and the circumstances of our lives are quite unlike Jesus' times, the anointing of God on our lives will look very different than Jesus' anointing.

13 Perhaps you will say something that helps another overcome years of fear. In that way, you have helped that person cast out their demons.

---

[1] NT Matthew 3:13-17
[2] NT Matthew 4:19
[3] NT Matthew 16:24
[4] NT First Corinthians 11:1

14 Perhaps your small kindness in someone's life gives them new hope. In this way, you may quite literally resurrect that person from the dead.

15 Perhaps you, listening to the Spirit within, will invent a new medical technology that heals thousands or millions of people. This will be one of the "greater things" Jesus promised we would do:

16 "I tell you the truth, anyone who has faith in me will do what I have been doing. He will do even greater things than these, because I am going to the Father."[1]

17 Jesus is our model, a subject to be followed.

18 Sadly, as we discussed in the Book of the Gospel, most people do not lead lives that matter.

19 Our lives are not Christ-like.

20 We are taught to let Jesus lead his important life *for* us, so we can get on with the small, fallen, meaningless lives that we spend all our time protecting.

21 The ways of old tell us we aren't responsible to feed the hungry because Jesus did it for us, and we don't need to help heal anyone because Jesus healed people for us.

22 We misunderstand when we think we can't be the ones to symbolically or literally help another be resurrected from death.

23 The notion of vicarious atonement has transformed Jesus the man, anointed by God, from a subject to be *followed* into an object to be *worshiped*.

Disregarding his call for us to love,
we think he alone was love.
Rejecting his insistence upon our perfection,
we think he alone was perfect.
Ignoring his call that we find our anointing,
we think he alone was the anointed of God.

24 We are taught to think it is enough that we simply *believe* Jesus did these things for us; nothing could possibly be further from the truth.

25 The life you live here and now *matters*.

26 You will not find fulfillment living your life vicariously through sports figures, movie stars or even Jesus of Nazareth.

27 You are here to become as he was and is: the Christ, the anointed of Yahweh.

28 You are here to heal, to inspire, to feed and to resurrect.

---

[1] NT John 14:12

29 You are even here to bear the sins of the world.[1]

30 This may be startling to you, but be assured: this is simply a return to the Gospel, the good news as it was originally preached:

> For us to become like Christ
> was Yahweh's divine plan
> from the very beginning.

31 The ways of old tell us, in ways overt and covert, that Jesus the perfect one lived a life no human could possibly emulate.

32 We are told over and over again that it isn't possible for us to "be perfect as our Father in heaven is perfect,"[2] and that's why Jesus was perfect *for* us, so that we could be perfect through belief in him.

33 The notion of vicarious living and atonement is absurd.

34 For far too long the delusion of vicarious living has prevented Yahweh's good people from becoming the Christ themselves.

35 Jesus plainly showed us how we should lead our lives.

36 We can, indeed, be perfect in the same way our Father in heaven is perfect. The blessed promise is that, eventually, we will be:

> "And after you have suffered for a little while,
> the God of all grace, who called you to
> His eternal glory in Christ,
> will Himself *perfect*, confirm,
> strengthen and establish you."

37 Human perfection is misunderstood.

38 Perfection does not mean you will never make another mistake.

39 A sapling is perfect, even though it grows to be a tree; an infant child is perfect, despite her youth.

40 The only requirement for the perfection Jesus speaks of is love: love for God, love for neighbors, and love for enemies.[3]

41 We are to learn humility, obedience, compassion and forgiveness—we are to *become* love.

42 Love is perfection.

43 The Spirit that lived in Jesus and anointed him as Christ desires to live in each of us.

44 Jesus was thousands of years ago, but Christ is now.

45 Christ is not far away; Christ is right here.

---

[1] FT Pain 4:11 - 20
[2] NT Matthew 5:48
[3] NT Matthew 5:44

46 Being you, the Christ, the anointed of God, is your true soul's destiny!

47 Christ is *here*. Christ is *now*. Anointed with the Holy Spirit, you are the Christ.

48 Christ formed in you is fulfillment.

49 In the end, there will be fulfillment.

50 The life that Jesus of Nazareth lived, anointed with the Holy Spirit of God, being the Christ, is our *example*. Follow it.

51 Jesus is our role model, teacher, guide and friend. Follow him.

52 Jesus, anointed with the Spirit that called him Christ, is a glimpse of the future you.

53 And the future you can emerge in *this* lifetime, *here* and *now*, not after you die or in another lifetime.

54 *All* he did, you will do, and more. Not in the same way, but it will be real.

55 You will feed the hungry, heal the sick, cast out demons and resurrect the dead, in astonishing ways beyond your imagination.

56 We are called to *follow* Jesus, not merely worship him.

57 Worshiping Jesus is a wonderful *beginning*, but worship is a means to an end, never an end in itself.

58 Worshiping Jesus for the sake of doctrinal purity means nothing.

59 The purpose of worshiping Christ is to imitate him and become like him.

60 The difference is profound.

Chapter 3
Born Again

1 Jesus said, "You must be born again."[1] What did he mean?

2 The first birth is earthly and fleshly. The first birth is the beginning of your social personality, our particular response to the "givens."

3 The specifics of our birth provide us with many givens: our parents, locale, language, family history, manners of eating, dress, language, politics, religion and financial values.

4 This is our first birth, to the world of flesh.

5 As we grow, our parents, schools, churches and social order expect that we internalize the givens.

---

[1] NT John 3:3

6 Conformity is the most highly valued social attribute.

7 We are social creatures: we want to gain approval and belong. So, over time, we begin to identify with our particular set of givens. That identification becomes our personality.

8 The small self, the personality, the ego, small mind, little will, carnal man: these are all descriptors of the narrow identification with the personal self conditioned by peer pressure.

9 In our culture, we identify with what we *do*, within the framework of societal expectations.

10 The eternal, limitless spirit within you is limited and identified as something the body is *doing*.

11 We have confused what we *do* with who we *are.*

12 Identifying with the social personality is the fundamental problem we must overcome.

13 The real purpose of Christianity and the Future Testament is to inspire us to rise above our identification with the old, fleshly "given" self.

14 We are to be re-born as the infant Christ and mature to the fulfillment of Christhood, the fruition of the Spirit.

15 Jesus commands us to follow him, to take up our crosses and move into eternal life with him, into the very same fulfillment and fruition of Christhood he found.

16 All aspects of the social personality (the "givens" of our birth) are bound in time and space. They are temporal, limited and cultural, and will therefore fall away, symbolically crucified on the cross of ego-transcendence.

17 The Infinite Spirit, beyond time and space, cannot be identified as lawyer or electrician or liberal or conservative.

18 Infinite Spirit, transcending time and space, can only be identified as God.

19 The genuine aim of religious life is to transform our consciousness from the small mind to the large mind, from the small ego to the limitless Spirit.

20 Like Jesus, we are to lay aside our little wills and follow the Will of God.

21 We, too, are called to embody "Not my will, but Thy Will be done."[1]

---

[1] NT Luke 22:42

22 No longer identifying with a socially conditioned personality, bound in time and space, you are free to identify with the Christ, to recognize that you *are* the Christ.

23 Saint Paul reveals what he calls the "mystery of the ages":

> "God gave me to present to you
> the word of God in its fullness—
> the mystery that has been kept
> hidden for ages and generations,
> but is now disclosed to the saints.
> To them God has chosen to
> make known among the Gentiles
> the glorious riches of this mystery,
> which is *Christ in you, the hope of glory.*"[1]

24 Paul's words are very clear. You can feel his excitement as he tells of this great mystery, the mystery which is, indeed, the source of all glorious riches: *Christ in you.*

25 The scripture does *not* say "*Jesus* in you," but "*Christ* in you."

26 Christ, the anointing of God, the infinite Spirit of God, came to reside in Jesus the man.[2] That same Spirit seeks to reside in every person on the Earth.

27 The deep need of every human, the proverbial hole in our hearts, is to move from the small "i" to the large "I," no longer identifying with the limited space-time personality, but knowing ourselves as the Christ.

28 Scandalous? Impossible? Not for Saint Paul.

29 That he was the Christ became the truth of Paul's life. It can become the central truth of *your* life.

30 Saint Paul was by no means born a saint, and he was certainly not born of a virgin. Paul spent years persecuting the church: he helped murder Christians[3] and did everything he could to imprison those who were proclaiming the message of the risen Lord. But when Paul met the risen Jesus on the Damascus road,[4] Jesus made it plain that the Christ desired to live in him.

31 Paul became a new man, born again to his Christ-self.

---

[1] NT Colossians 1: 25–27
[2] NT Matthew 3:16 & 17
[3] NT Acts 8:1 - 3
[4] NT Acts 9

32 As he grew in his perfection, Saint Paul was able to say "It is no longer I who live, but Christ who lives in me!"[1]

33 Paul no longer identified with his small "i," his earthly mind, his ego or his personality of "givens;" Saint Paul recognized the truth of himself as the Christ.

34 Paul, the new man in Christ, now accounted all of his awards, degrees, accomplishments and worldly successes as being worthless in comparison to the anointing of God, the Christ within him.[2]

35 Indeed, the only thing that matters in life is being able to recognize that you are part of God, an extension of God and indeed, one with God. God is love, even love of enemies, and that is perfection.

36 We move from the small "i" of human love to the large "I" of Divine Love.

37 The only worthwhile goal is to recognize that the Christ lives in you.

38 God is here. God is now.

39 You are part of God; God is in you. You are Christ. Your life's fruition is to recognize you are no longer society's small ego, but rather the Living Anointing of God, the Christ. In this is the fruit of the Spirit, perfect love, joy and peace.

40 You need to be free to live without conforming to society's expectations, or even your parents'.

41 Is this still too scandalous and shocking? Paul continues, talking about his disciples being like children with whom he is in labor until "Christ is formed in you."[3]

42 When you are born again, what are you born again *into*? You are born into real spirituality. You become conscious of who you *really* are; the Spirit of Christ within is quickened and begins to grow.

43 The Christ within eventually fills you completely. Christ is formed in you. You live as the Christ.

44 You no longer identify with the small ego, but with the Christ who lives in and through you. Me. Us. Everyone.

45 Lamentably, even thousands of years after Paul revealed it openly, the mystery of the ages remains a mystery.

46 Most Christian churches aren't proclaiming it.

---

[1] NT Galatians 2:20
[2] NT Philippians 3:1 - 11
[3] NT Galatians 4:19

47 Certainly, government and commerce don't want you to know the truth, because if you live as Christ in the flesh, you do not need a government to tell you what to do.

48 If you are Christ, you no longer look to commerce to tell you what to want.

49 Notice how directly these ideas connect to the Books of Fulfillment and Liberty, the first books of the Future Testament.

50 The books of the Future Testament are really different aspects of *one* thing, like looking at a precious diamond from different perspectives. Even though you can see each facet in its individuality, you are looking at one thing:

> Liberty is directly connected to
> Scripture, Gospel and Christ.
> This is your Fulfillment.

51 Now we can see more clearly why Jesus said we have to carry our own crosses.

52 Your cross is the vehicle upon which your socialized ego "i" will be slain, so that you can rise to the new life in the Spirit.

53 Your cross is unique to you:

> Perhaps your cross is a lifetime of selfless service
> or pathways of prayer and meditation,
> maybe mental study and contemplation,
> or loving dedication to worshiping God in Jesus,
> or possibly your cross will be some failure,
> like divorce, addiction or disease.

54 When you are ready, God will provide the living lessons that will form your cross.

55 The Christ greatly desires to be born in you and will find a way to get your attention.

56 The Christ desires to live as you.

57 But be warned: taking up your cross and following Christ to infinite glory is the most precious and serious of commitments. Being born again is no game.

58 God is not fooled. There is no "partial" Christhood.

59 The Christ cannot live in parallel with selfishness, greed, hatred or even indifference.

60 All that is not Christ-like will be purged from your being as you grow to fulfillment.

61 The Christ is mercy, compassion, love and humility.

62 The Christ is perfect, even as God is perfect.

Chapter 4
The Fruit of the Spirit

1 Jesus of Nazareth was a living Tree of Life. Speaking as the Christ, he said as much: "I am the vine; you are the branches. If a man remains in me and I in him, he will bear much fruit; apart from me you can do nothing."[1]

2 Jesus, anointed as the Christ, perfectly exemplified the fruit of the Spirit.

3 Jesus was love, joy, peace, patience, kindness, goodness, faithfulness, gentleness and self-control.[2]

4 He had to come to the fruition of his soul through the anointing presence of the Holy Spirit.

5 When he said, "Not my will, but Thy will be done," he perfectly expressed how we move from the small "i" to the large "I."

6 We must travel the same path. Jesus cannot do for us what we are unwilling to do for ourselves.

7 Our free will allows us, in all circumstances, to operate from selfishness or love.

8 We cannot "remain in him [Christ] and bear much fruit"[3] if we remain caught in ego, in our small mind.

9 The world is in need of the fruit of the Spirit.

10 This is why the Future Testament emphasizes that Jesus is not an object to be *worshiped*, but is a subject to be *followed*: Jesus of Nazareth, fully man and fully God, embodied the living Holy Spirit. As the Christ, he lived the fruit of the Spirit.

11 He taught us that real peace, the peace of the Spirit, overcomes hatred, killing and war.

12 Your liberation is none other than being born again, to become the living, risen Christ.

13 Look to yourself as being a miniature God in the flesh. "Jesus answered them, 'Is it not written in your law, I said, Ye are gods?'"[4]

---

[1] NT John 5:5
[2] NT Galatians 5:22 & 23
[3] NT John 15:5
[4] NT John 10:34

14 It is your goal to be as Jesus was. It is your goal to be perfect, as your Father in heaven is perfect.

15 Open yourself to the Presence of the Spirit. The anointing of the Christ will be quickened within you and will fill you completely.

16 The Holy Spirit of Christ, which has begun a good work in you, will perfect it.[1]

Chapter 5
I Am the Way, the Truth and the Life

1 Jesus said, "I am the way, the truth and the life. No one comes to the Father but by me."[2]

2 This is one of the most misunderstood and misused verses in the Bible.

3 You may have heard the first half of the verse quoted ad infinitum, most frequently at Resurrection Sunday services; the second half of the verse is rarely mentioned in New Age churches.

4 The Future Testament affirms the truth of Jesus' words in their fullness. The Future Testament seeks to fulfill these words. But what do they mean?

5 "I am the way, the truth and the life. No one comes to the Father but by me" does *not* mean that you must believe that Jesus died to pay the penalty for your sins.

6 Fulfillment of the cross is not a doctrine to *believe* but a reality to *live*.

7 God is here, God is now.

8 Heaven is here and now. You will not go to heaven after you die if you are living a life identified with the smallness of ego; you will carry all of your enmity, greed and resentments into your own self-fashioned hell.

9 To "come to the Father" means to have Christ fully formed in *you*.

10 To "come to the Father" is the same thing as "Not my will, but Thy will be done."

11 To "come to the Father" means to find our personal perfection, our fruition, the embodiment of the fruit of the Spirit.

12 What does it mean when Jesus said, "I am the way"?

---

[1] NT Philippians 1:6
[2] NT John 14:6

13 We need a pathway.

14 We need a map or a trail to guide us on the grand journey. Someone needs to show us how to travel from where we are (in our limited, ego-filled space-time "i") to the fulfillment of Christ formed in us.

15 We need help: a path and a guide. Jesus was the trail-blazer.

16 The way of the cross is the path. The life Jesus lived is the guide.

17 Take up your cross and follow him. There are many methods but *only one way*!

18 You can devote your life to selfless work, heartfelt devotion, feeding the poor, meditation, prayer, contemplation; all of these revolve around the same essence: taking up your cross and following him.

> There is only one way to
> "come to the Father,"
> and that is for your ego to
> die upon your personal cross.

19 Falsehood clamors for your attention, but truth stands quietly victorious.

20 Test, examine and live, that the real, glorious truth is this:

21 God is here. God is now. The kingdom of God is within you. The kingdom of God is in our midst. This is the pearl of great price.

22 Incarnating the Spirit of God is the true life.

23 Truth is the only religion.

24 Crucifying ego upon the cross of time is the only *way* to experience the *truth* of *life*.

25 Your ego-self will die.

26 You will *not* identify with your social conditioning for the rest of eternity.

27 You won't have your body for the rest of eternity.

28 You will not identify with your biological parents for eternity.

29 The only eternal identity is the Spirit of God, the Christ within.

30 The Christ is *outside* time and space yet is forever involved *inside* time and space.

31 Your life as Christ is the only life that is eternal.

32 Your life as Christ is the only life worthy of your identification.

33 Christ is formed in us as we transcend our notions about the small "i" and embrace our true "I," the Christ. That's when we are born again.

34 Jesus is speaking as the Christ. To paraphrase, Jesus the Christ is saying "I, the Christ, am the only way to the Father. This is the only truth, and this is the only life. No one comes to the Father but by embodying me, the Christ consciousness, by dying to self and rising to the anointing of God within."

35 You may be surprised or shocked to learn this: becoming the Christ is possible even for people who have not heard the name "Jesus."

36 It is possible for Buddhists, Hindus, Muslims and Sikhs. It is possible for people in pre-industrialized lands.

37 This is what Paul meant when he said, "When the people of the world do the things of the law without the written Hebrew law, they become a law to themselves."[1]

38 The Spirit of God is always working on the hearts of men and women everywhere.

39 Throughout the ages, continents and centuries, all beings are capable of living selfishly, growing their ego-self at the expense of everyone else, or they can transcend ego, becoming a servant of the one true God, regardless of their language.

40 In any social order, you can always live according to the small self or the large self.

41 A journey through unknown territory is always easier with a path and a guide. And we have been given a glorious path and a wonderful guide to the one way, the one truth and the one life: the way of the cross and the life Jesus lived as the Christ.

Chapter 6
Sons and Daughters

1 Christians put Jesus on a pedestal, as someone fundamentally different, better and smarter than themselves.

2 People worship Jesus so they can ignore his advice.

3 The ways of old want you to believe Jesus was fundamentally different so you will ignore his guidance.

4 But Jesus called us friends.[2] After we are all fully instructed, he said, we shall be equal to our teacher.[3]

---

[1] NT Romans 2:14
[2] NT John 15:15
[3] NT Luke 6:40

5 Even after his resurrection from the dead, Jesus sought to emphasize the similarities between us, not any apparent differences.

6 He said it as plainly as he could: "Behold, I go to *my* Father and *your* Father, to *my* God and *your* God."[1]

7 Jesus made no distinction between us and himself, except that he is at the head of the class in the schoolwork of life, the able teacher ready to lead the way to resurrection.

8 God is our Father in the same way He is Jesus' Father.

9 Jesus never even implied that we are *adopted.*

10 We are *indeed* the children of God, in the same way Jesus was.

11 Jesus was the forerunner. He blazed the trail we are to follow, the way of transcending ego. He was the first to identify with his Christ-self, and he constantly invited us to join him as equals.

12 You too are the begotten child of God.

13 We are all children of God.

14 As the scripture says, "For you are all sons and daughters of God."[2]

15 The ultimate truth is God is here; God is now.

16 God is in us.

17 We are Christ.

18 As the scripture says, "Be imitators of God, therefore, as dearly loved children."[3]

19 After the first birth, children imitate their parents, teachers and friends.

20 After the new birth we imitate the Holy Spirit.

21 Children imitate those who they love. Imitation is a learning, growing experience.

22 As the Holy Spirit descended upon Jesus in his baptism and descended as tongues of fire on the apostles, the Holy Spirit desires to descend upon you.

23 The anointing of God wasn't just for Jesus and his followers a long time ago.

24 The anointing of God is here and now, waiting to elevate you and every person on the Earth.

25 Divinity's Children, join the song of resurrection:

---

[1] NT John 20:17
[2] NT Galatians 3:26
[3] NT Ephesians 5:1

Jesus was God in the flesh,
and so are you.
Imitate him.
Jesus was Yahweh's child,
and so are you.
Imitate him.
Jesus experienced the indwelling
Christ as his true self,
and so can you.
Imitate him.
Jesus died to sin when he said
"Not my will, but Thy Will be done."
Imitate him.
Jesus invites you to carry your cross,
to follow him on the pathway to
his God and *our* God, to *his* Father and *our* Father.
Imitate him.
There is no other *way* to find the fruition of your soul.
There is no other pathway to perfection.
There is no other *truth*.
There is no other *life*.
Divinity's Children, celebrate your birthright.
Be who and what you *really* are.
Unite with Christ Jesus through faith,
the faith that all of this is true,
the faith that unites us with the
life he lived and the deeds he did,
the faith that unites us with him
in the death of ego
and the faith that unites us in
the resurrection to new life.

26 Be imitators of God as beloved children until the day that Christ is fully formed in you. This is your fruition, your liberty. This is your birthright. You are the Christ. This is the heart of the Gospel.

The Future Testament

Book Eight: The Book of Salvation

Chapter 1
Beginning Once Again

1 Our notions about salvation are too small.

2 "Salvation" means to salve, to heal, to fix.

3 Simply put, when you are completely healed, then you are saved.

4 In order to understand salvation, we must understand humanity's sickness, our sin.

5 In the book of Genesis, it is clear that everything God makes is very good.[1]

6 God gives Adam and Eve perfect freedom to go everywhere in the Garden of Eden. They were encouraged to eat from every tree, except for one certain tree: the Tree of Knowledge of Good and Evil.[2]

7 This was not a *test*, but a *warning*.

8 Although everything God created was good, there is something called the Tree of Knowledge of Good and *Evil*.

9 If everything is *good*, then what is *evil*?

10 In order to have the knowledge of both good *and* evil, Adam and Eve had to have knowledge of everything that existed (good) and *things that did not exist (evil)*, like pain, jealousy, enmity, murder and disease.

11 God warned Adam and Eve to stay away from this tree because *it could hurt them.*

12 Yahweh prohibited the tree not as a test, but as a warning.

13 Yet, as must always happen, Adam and Eve ate from the tree; immediately their eyes were opened. Their consciousness changed.

14 This was not just *any* tree, chosen arbitrarily as a test; rather, this tree had the ability to change their consciousness!

15 They saw not only what they *were*, but what they were *not*.

16 And they were *not* clothed.

17 Before partaking of the forbidden fruit, their nakedness was a source of celebration, a part of the goodness of the Universe.

---

[1] OT Genesis 1, verses 4, 10, 12, 18, 21, 25 and 31
[2] OT Genesis 2:17

18 After their proverbial eyes were opened, they saw not only what they *were*, their bodies, (which were good) but also what they were *not*, and they were not clothed. They perceived this as evil.

19 They experienced shame.

20 This changed awareness, turning from what *is* to what *is not*, was the original sin.

21 Disobedience was *not* the original sin. Yes, they disobeyed, but no, that was not their sin. Disobedience lead to their sin, which was a harmful way of looking at life.

22 Disobedience is always a means to an end, never an end in itself.

23 The essence of Adam and Eve's sin was the separation of their consciousness from the pure state of all goodness.

24 Sin is separation. "To sin" is to sunder, break, fracture.

25 When we sin, we miss the mark; the connection is not made.

26 Adam and Eve went from being at one with creation, Creator and each other to a separation of consciousness, which blocked them from the goodness all around them.

27 Symbolically, they "hid" from the Creator. Sin hides us from the Creator.

28 The light of the Universe that was to flow from the Creator, through them, into the creation, became broken.

29 The change of consciousness, knowing good and evil,[1] caused the circuit to break.

30 Ego separation had entered the Universe.

31 Adam's first statement after the fall is most telling, full of ego: "*I* heard the sound of Thee in the garden, and *I* was afraid because *I* was naked, so *I* hid *myself*."[2]

32 The unitive state of universal goodness had been fractured into mine and not mine, yours and not yours, ours and not ours.

33 Ego was created, along with all of the pain and suffering that would grow from shattering the oneness of goodness and love.

34 In response, Genesis tells us that God cast Adam and Eve out of the Garden.[3] The ways of old misunderstand this as *punishment*.

35 The truth is that by banning Adam and Eve from the Garden, God was preventing a far worse fate for them.

---

[1] OT Genesis 3:22
[2] OT Genesis 3:10
[3] OT Genesis 3:24

36 Their banishment was a small hurt they could feel in order to prevent a much larger one they could not imagine. This is the very definition of *loving* discipline.

37 If, in their fallen state, they had been allowed to eat from the Tree of Life, then their pain, sorrow, suffering and ego would have been *touched with eternal life.*[1] *Misery itself would have been immortalized.*

38 Their knowledge of good and evil, and thus *our* knowledge of good and evil, would have been the constant state of consciousness for the rest of eternity. Salvation would not be possible.

39 But pain is not forever.[2] Misery does not last. All sin will die away,[3] leaving only love, joy and goodness.

40 Disobedience was never the issue.

Chapter 2
Discipline and Punishment

1 It is impossible for you to love your children more than Yahweh loves you.

2 Always remember, through all your religious deliberations and spiritual growth, that God is our loving, heavenly Father and Mother.

3 If you warn your child not to touch the hot stove, the child's disobedience is a *secondary* problem that leads to the *primary* problem: your child might be badly burned.

4 Real punishment cannot be eternal or absolute.

5 Loving parental discipline inflicts a lesser pain that *can* be understood to prevent a greater pain that *cannot* be understood.

6 The slap to your child's hand that stops her from touching a hot fire is a lesser pain that avoids an unimaginable tragedy.

7 Would your Father in heaven's divine punishment be any less loving than your own parental guidance?

8 Anything else is vengeance and retribution. The Future Testament declares that such characteristics, ascribed to our God, are abhorrent to His very nature. And ours.

---

[1] OT Genesis 3:22
[2] FT Pain 7:9 - 16
[3] NT Romans 6:23

9 God was *disciplining* Adam and Eve when he made them leave the Garden. He was *not* striking them in anger for their disobedience.

10 Discipline is correction, education and training.

11 Discipline is always a means to an end, never an end in itself.

12 God knew Adam and Eve had to toil, sweat, learn and grow their way back to the unitive consciousness of Paradise.

13 Yahweh knew that Adam and Eve needed to receive the love lessons necessary to overcome ego before they could return to the Tree of Life.

14 At the end of the New Testament, mankind, having overcome its problems of ego through uniting with Christ, is once again able to partake from the Tree of Life, eternally returning to our primordial state of bliss:

> "Blessed are those who
> wash their robes, that
> they may have the right
> to the Tree of Life."[1]

15 The Future Testament deeply desires to help fulfill this prophecy; it is the one and only thing worth striving for.

16 Since disobedience was not the problem, then the idea that God needed Jesus' death to pay a bloody penalty for our "disobedience" becomes meaningless.

17 The notion of God watching His son bleed, suffer and die in order to appease His wrath against us, the offending sinners, is absurd and offensive.

18 The ways of old would have us believe that God had to pay a bloody penalty *to* Himself, *by* Himself, *for* crimes *against* Himself.

19 Note carefully: salvation, as imagined by the ways of old, is a manifestation of the ego-fractured mindset that conceived it.

20 Rather, the fruit of the Tree of Knowledge of Good and Evil contained a psychic poison, for which God had to create an antidote.

21 Partaking of this fruit changed Adam and Eve's way of thinking. It created a split in consciousness that expressed duality (you vs. me, God vs. us) and destroyed the organic oneness of the beginning.

22 Yahweh's antidote to the poison of ego was expressed most clearly in Jesus the Christ.

---

[1] NT Revelation 22:14

23 The life of Christ is essential to healing the poison of ego. Taking up our crosses and following Christ is the active agent in the antidote.

24 The original sin is the existence of a separate ego operating against the Divine.

25 The solution is precisely what the Future Testament speaks of in the Books of the Gospel and Christ: re-think your life, take up your cross, and transcend ego. "You must be born again."[1]

26 From the depths of our souls, we must say with our elder brother Jesus, "Not my will, but Thy will be done."[2]

27 Ego says, "I want things my way." Again, sin is "missing the mark." When ego dies, we *hit* the mark, reconnecting to God. Then we become vessels of God's will.

28 Not my way, but Yahweh.

29 Return to the unitive state of love, as the Christ you really are. This is your fulfillment and fruition. This is the meaning of the cross, the message of Christ and your salvation.

Chapter 3
True Salvation

1 Since there was no penalty to be paid, but only a condition to be overcome, then Jesus cannot do for us what we must do for ourselves.

2 Jesus was not the atonement for your sins.

3 Jesus' sacrifice, his pathway to Golgotha, does us no good if we are not willing to *follow him* by dying to ego.

4 Salvation, then, cannot possibly be one moment, one event, or even one decision.

5 True salvation is deliverance, healing, being made whole.

6 Thus, only when you are made whole are you truly saved.

7 When we turn in repentance, saying "God help me," at that moment all sin is forgiven.

8 Yahweh's love and forgiveness are constant, like a loving mother. Our repentance allows us to *receive* what is *always there*.

9 But forgiveness is never an end in itself, only a means to an end.

10 When we honestly change our minds and turn to the light, God is there to forgive.

---

[1] NT John 3:3
[2] NT Luke 22:42

11 Such an event is certainly a moment of celebration, but it is only a beginning.

12 Much healing is necessary for a soul's lost life to be made whole.

13 Salvation is when you are whole.

14 God's infinite love will accept nothing less than your fruition, the Spirit living perfectly through you. Only that fulfillment can be called true salvation.

15 A life spent dedicated to the I/me/my of ego cannot possibly be made whole by reciting a prescribed prayer one time in a conversion moment.

16 Conversion is a means to an end, never an end in itself.

17 You are made whole, truly saved, when *all* the effects of sin and ego have been repaired and you are restored to spiritual health.

18 No parent could be content with less.

19 We are only made whole when we have been restored to union with God.

> Real salvation is
> the Book of Fulfillment.
> The pathway to salvation is
> the Book of the Gospel,
> expressed in the Book of Christ.
> They are all aspects of
> the unitive experience
> of Love with God.
> Goodness is how we were made
> and where we are going.

20 Anything else packaged as "salvation" is a phony substitute for the truth, a false prophet trying to assuage your guilt, often for the sake of controlling you and gaining access to your money.

21 There is no salvation short of expressing Christ in the flesh. Your flesh, my flesh, all flesh.

22 To be the Christ is wholeness.

23 We struggle until Christ is formed in all of us.

24 True salvation is magnificently embodied in the New Testament:

"We should always give thanks to God for you,
brothers and sisters beloved of the Lord,
because God has chosen you from the beginning
for salvation through sanctification by
the Spirit and faith in the truth. It was for
this he called you through our Gospel that you
may gain the glory of our Lord Jesus Christ."[1]

25 Salvation is gaining the glory of Christ. That's when you are delivered, protected, healed, preserved and made whole.

26 Salvation comes through being made holy, free from sin, by the Spirit of God.

27 What else can make us holy and free from sin but to become like Christ?

28 Salvation and sanctification are the same thing, and there are no substitutes.

29 Your salvation is your sanctification, which is Christ formed in you.

Chapter 4
Salvation Is Fulfillment

1 In the end, there will be fulfillment.[2]

2 In the end, there will be salvation.

3 "Christ Jesus came into the world to *save* sinners."[3]

4 Christ came to save sinners, but his saving is not arbitrary, nor is it a ceremonious ritual.

5 Christ's saving is an abiding reality.

6 The Christ is our savior. The Christ was Jesus' savior.

7 Christ came to save those caught in the sin of ego.

8 This kind of *saving* is precisely what the Book of Christ expresses.

9 In order to find eternal life, to be made whole, the small "i" of ego must be transcended.

---

[1] NT Second Thessalonians 2:13 & 14
[2] FT Fulfillment 1:1
[3] NT First Timothy 1:15

10 The small self, identifying with the givens of family, history, culture and language, must die.

11 We must lose our small lives in order to find eternal life.

12 The only truth is the infinite, eternal God.

13 Truth is the only religion.

14 "Those who seek to save their life will lose it."[1] The person who clings to the small life, making it their existence, will lose everything they hold dear.

15 Life dedicated to the "i" of ego is a life disconnected from God. It is a life of separation, and separation from God was the original sin of Adam and Eve.

16 Separation from God underpins all other sin.

17 Salvation is returning to identification with God.

18 We are saved from separation and return to oneness.

19 "For it is by grace you have been saved, through faith—and this not from yourselves, it is the gift of God…"[2]

20 God anoints Divinity's Children with His Spirit, restoring Paradise.

21 This happens through grace.

22 We are saved by grace; that is the gift of God.

23 God is the only lasting reality.

24 Yahweh's grace is the living, moving, breathing action of Yahweh's Holy Spirit. It is vibrant and essential to the growth of the Spirit within.

25 Grace actively works with our beliefs, touching them and turning them into faith.

26 Faith grows toward the Presence of God as flowers look toward the Sun.

27 As you live in accordance with the precepts of love, service and sacrifice, no longer identified with the small "i" of ego but fully identified with the large "I" of the Christ within, you are whole. You are saved.

28 Christ fully formed in you is your real salvation.

29 To see the commonality of all people rather than the differences; to know what makes us one instead of what makes us separate; to feel, see and know our oneness with God: this is salvation.

30 This is loving God and loving each other: the Law is salvation.

31 We are saved by grace, and through faith we are made whole.

---

[1] NT Luke 17:33
[2] NT Ephesians 2:8

The Future Testament

Book Nine: The Book of Grace

Chapter 1
Ideas Grow and Change

1 Our notions about grace are too small.

2 The concept of grace has gone through centuries of change.

3 By means of language and education, we can chart the development of different ideas through time.

4 Every one of the concepts discussed in the Future Testament has gone through a series of changes and developments, growth and maturation.

5 Most of the ideas have proven in their youth to have been well-guided but ultimately misinformed.

6 We prefer to say that mistaken ideas are "young" rather than "evil."

7 A child's mistaken thought cannot be called evil, because to have an evil thought implies a mature ability to be willful.

8 However, time and new information have shown us that some of our ideas have clearly been wrong. It is wise to think of these erroneous thoughts as young, the best efforts of a child–like humanity growing, looking, exploring, and trying to understand the ways of life and truth.

9 The Future Testament calls such ideas "the ways of old."

10 It is the hope of the Future Testament that the process of growth continues until the human race has come to its fruition, when the human race is entirely free, none are slaves, and all are finding salvation in being the embodiment of Christ, according to the scriptures of their choosing.

11 Over the course of time, we will come to discover that we are all fingers on the glorious hand of Divinity. We are all players in the same Divine play. Each and every one of us matters and has something to contribute to the Divine whole.

12 Similarly, our individual thoughts are all part of the Divine mind, information essential to the Divine play.

13 Individuals and ideas only find their true value in relationship to each other.

14 The twelve books of the Future Testament are all interrelated, each finding illumination and clarification in the others.

15 Our notions of liberty are connected to scripture, which are connected to our ideas about Christ and salvation, which are connected to all the others.

16 Because our ideas are connected, as one idea changes, all the other ideas change.

17 Growth in one area leads to growth in all.

18 As our notions of salvation and Christ grow, our notions about grace, freedom and faith change as well.

19 Each is connected to all.

20 As our notions of ourselves mature, so do our ideas of God.

21 There are some notions of grace that we can now acknowledge as being part of humanity's youth.

Chapter 2
The Old Testament

1 In the Old Testament, grace was equivalent to Yahweh's favor.

2 Grace was most commonly seen as the granting of material blessings. If you had Yahweh's grace, you would live a long life.

3 If you had Yahweh's favor, the Sun would shine, the rain would come in perfect proportion, and your crops would grow lush and bountiful.[1]

4 A village with Yahweh's favor was protected and able to crush all foes, so the people could live in happiness and prosperity.

5 In the Old Testament, every person knew the role they played in order to receive Yahweh's favor. The Jews, Yahweh's chosen people, were expected to follow Yahweh's commandments. In the first five books of the Bible, the Torah, there are 613 commandments as to what the Jews must do and not do.

6 Keeping those commandments, it was promised, would lead to Yahweh's grace and prosperity, peace and long life.

7 Breaking a commandment, or simply failing to keep any one of Yahweh's commandments, was guaranteed to bring calamity. One

---

[1] OT Deuteronomy 11:13 - 15

8 mistake and you were responsible for affecting the amount of rain the land received that year. Your actions were what determined how pleased God would be with you and your community.

9 This thinking quickly led to a ritualistic approach to righteousness. A long list of festivals, and instructions about keeping the festivals, developed to form the calendar of the Jewish people.

10 Ritual sacrifices of animals and gifts of grain were offered up to God in attempts to atone for sin and to request Yahweh's forgiveness for the inevitable breaking of commandments.

11 The people believed they were required to perform perfectly in order for God to grant His grace.

12 When the Hebrews sinned against God, there were different procedures to go through so they might be washed clean, forgiven, and returned to Yahweh's favor.

13 The lives of the children depended upon the morality of their parents: how well or how poorly they kept Yahweh's commandments and whether they pleased or displeased Him.

14 The Old Testament prophets spent much time telling people they were in danger of great calamity because they had forsaken Yahweh and His ways.

15 The Old Testament people struggled to determine what Yahweh truly required:

16 The Torah established many ceremonies and sacrifices, but Hosea and Amos said that God wanted nothing to do with those animal sacrifices, rituals and ceremonies; what God really wanted was a loving, contrite heart full of mercy toward one's fellow human beings.[1]

17 The difference between *real* religion (acting lovingly, showing kindness and goodness) and the *substitute* religion of sacrificial ceremonies is a constant theme throughout the writings of the Old Testament prophets.

18 In the Old Testament, Yahweh's grace was an external favor, earned by real or ceremonial performance.

---

[1] OT Hosea 6:6, Amos 5:21 - 24

Chapter 3
The New Testament

1 By the time of the New Testament, the notion of Yahweh's grace had shifted dramatically.

2 Life had proven exceedingly hard for the Jews, after more than a thousand years of following Yahweh's laws and atoning for their failures of performance.

3 The Jews had been dominated and conquered by many armies, and at the time of Jesus' life, they were an occupied territory. Rome completely possessed Jerusalem and the land of Palestine.

4 Since Earthly life had been so difficult for so long, the Jews began to look for hope elsewhere, outside the realms of material blessing.

5 Over the course of time, the notion of Yahweh's grace left the Earth plane and became centered upon the next world.

6 The people had begun to believe life was going to consist of suffering, misery and death, whether or not they followed Yahweh's commandments. Bad things were still going to happen, regardless of performance. There would still be sickness, famine and death. Invading armies were still going to kill them whether or not they were faithful to all 613 Old Testament commandments.

7 This is the central thesis of the Book of Job. Job has done everything right his whole life. He has been a good, faithful and obedient person, and yet horror still comes to him.

8 So, the quest for Yahweh's grace shifted from finding Yahweh's favor on Earth to seeking eternal favor in the next world.

9 Granted, life was suffering and misery, but your suffering and misery could lead to one of two conclusions: die in your suffering and go to hell for an eternity, or die with Yahweh's grace and be granted heavenly reward.

10 The Jews began to seek Yahweh's grace in the afterlife.

11 They began to think their reward was to be found in the afterlife. For the New Testament writers, the question became what to do in order to gain Yahweh's favor of eternal life.

12 In the time of Jesus of Nazareth, the people of Yahweh were obsessed with the survival of one's individual soul.

13 Initially, people listened to Jesus. His words of instruction *mattered*.

14 Eventually, however, the wonderful words he spoke, the parables he taught, the miracles he performed and the life he lived *no longer mattered.*

15 To the ways of old, all Jesus taught and did in life became inconsequential compared to what he did in dying.

16 Ignorantly, the church began to teach that by believing Jesus' death had vicariously absorbed God's wrath, grace was now available to all. Yahweh's so-called grace, the gift of eternal life in heaven, could now be given freely to all human beings, because God had exacted the penalty for our disobedience on His own son.

17 To the ways of old, Jesus died upon the cross to pay the penalty for all sin. Now, all people were invited to come into heaven simply on the basis of believing in the atoning sacrifice of Jesus.

18 From these young ideas was born the acronym G-R-A-C-E: God's Riches At Christ's Expense.

19 The young theology was simple-minded: God gave Jesus what we deserve in order to give us what Jesus deserved.

20 Sadly, this idea became the cornerstone of Christianity.

21 In the context of history, it can be explained but, like slavery, never justified.

Chapter 4
Humanity Grows Up, a Little

1 The Old and New Testament notions of grace are not to be thought *wrong* so much as *young.*

2 In the beginning, God seemed to be wholly other and completely separate from everything human and earthly.

3 Humans sought to find Yahweh's favor, thinking that the God who is above and beyond will reach down and make good things happen for us if we please Him. The idea persists today.

4 Youthful humanity was constantly reaching out to various gods in an effort to appease them and seek favor, but life was difficult. The Earthly world began to lose its luster.

5 We began to experience this world as a stepping stone to the next, seeking to assure our place in heaven when we die. This became the meaning of grace.

6 Time passed. We entered the so-called Enlightenment, followed by the "Death of God" movement, but things did not get any better.

7 In modern times, the official scientific cosmology is that energy/mass is the ultimate reality, and there is no God, no soul and no next world.

8 Humanity has returned to where it began: looking for joy on Earth before being snuffed out; only this time, there is no God of grace.

9 Modern grace is found in consumerism fueled by science.

10 Post-enlightenment mankind turned to chemical science, government and corporations for salvation.

11 Eventually, the New Age movement said that the opposite of the modern cosmology is true: we ourselves are God.

12 New Thought teaches there is no God transcendent; there is only God immanent, and we are all, each of us, God.

13 These modern denominations teach that problems arise simply because we have the wrong thoughts, ideas, affirmations or confessions.

14 This is an idea that is virtually indistinguishable from the ancient Jewish thought that even the rain is controlled by our obedience to Yahweh's commands.

15 God may have been taken out of the New Age equation, but the net result is the same.

16 Meanwhile, much of humanity, tired of the struggle, vainly holds to the ancient ideas of vicarious atonement.

17 Much like survivors adrift in the ocean will hold onto anything that floats, post-nuclear Christianity holds fervently to salvation at the expense of one man's suffering 2,000 years ago.

18 Both the youthful ideas of the past and the misinterpretations of modernity are incomplete notions about the beauty of real grace.

19 Our ideas about self, God, grace and favor are all linked, and they are all too small.

Chapter 5
Grace Is Life

1 Our notions about grace are too small.

2 The Future Testament invites you to test, examine and live: grace is not the child-like idea of finding Yahweh's blessings in the physical plane; nor is Yahweh's grace found in believing your salvation comes through a sacrificial substitute to gain favor in the next world.

3 Everything here is different. Everything.

4 Grace is so much more than our weak imaginations of the past ever allowed.

5 Grace is not the power that enables you to have a good life: *grace is life itself.*

6 When you can move your fingers, hear a cat's purr, see your baby smile, wonder at the miracle of a hummingbird, be astonished at the depth and complexity of subatomic structures, become overwhelmed with the incomprehensible beauty of mathematics… all of these, and so many more, are grace.

7 Grace enables you to think. Grace enables you to feel. Grace enables you to love.

8 Grace is, in fact, your life.

9 And yet, grace is not an unmerited favor.

10 Real grace is the very Heart of God.

11 Grace is the very purpose of your existence.

12 What mother, holding her newborn close to nurse, could look at her child and say, "You do not deserve the nourishment I am giving you from my body"?

13 What parent, providing a warm bed and a playroom for his child, would think it "unmerited favor" or "your riches at my expense"?

14 Always remember the notion of God as loving heavenly father, nursing mother.

15 A parent is not estranged from us but intimately connected with us.

16 The love we have for our precious babies is but a hint of the infinite love the God of the Universe has for Divinity's Children.

17 The mother–child relationship, as intimate as it is, nevertheless expresses itself as a degree of separation.

18 You are even more connected to God than you could possibly be to your own nursing infant.

19 You are not, and could never be, separated from God.

20 We are not only the children of God, but even more: we are the very blood cells that course through Yahweh's body.

21 We are not separate from God; we are directly connected to God.

22 We live in God; we move around in God; our very existence is inside of God.[1]

23 We are not made of anything other than God Himself.

24 From the beginning of time, nothing has ever been created or destroyed; things only change form.

25 Creation is just an illusion.

26 God is the everything from which all comes, of which all consists.

27 We are each a tiny part of the great cosmic God.

28 For a season, a tiny part of God has been turned into the form called "you."

29 We bubble off the face of eternity, as blood cells are born of bone marrow to serve their purpose.

30 Your blood cells are not made of anything other than your body.

31 Your body does not belong to your neighbor or your goldfish or your cat or the president; it belongs to you.

32 Your body is, intimately and only, made up of you. And yet, you are much more than simply your collection of blood cells.

33 This is where the modern ideas get it wrong: it is not true that there is no God, nor is it true that we are the only God there is.

34 We are indeed God, a part of God, but God *is not us*.

35 Yahweh's grace is not a matter of finding favor, regardless of performance or merit. Such ideas are too small and belong in our past.

36 Yahweh's grace is to recognize the sacred, eternal divinity which is ours.

37 The mother praises the child for every step he takes, even though he has much left to learn. This is not unmerited favor: this is love.

38 Remember that the young child is perfect, even with much to learn; God sees you the same way!

39 The body celebrates the goodness of all the cells that perform their duties, not as a matter of unmerited favor, but as an expression of life's miracle; God celebrates you the same way!

40 Speak not, then, of Yahweh's grace as being something *given* to you, for by your very existence you *are* Yahweh's grace!

41 Think not, then, of Yahweh's grace as being granted to you on the basis of Jesus' suffering; God's grace is your birthright.

---

[1] NT Acts 17:28

42 Grace is your divine identity.

43 Eventually, we will know as much about God as God knows about us, which is everything.[1]

44 Christ, the fullness of God, will be formed in us.

45 Every generation thinks it has the ultimate answers to life's mysteries. So it has been for thousands of years.

46 Do not limit Yahweh's grace by merely thinking His grace allows you into heaven when you die.

47 Grace is about life, not death.

48 If you are caught in ego, pain, misery and hatred, then forgiveness is simply not the point.

49 Your soul will carry its ego, pain, misery and hatred into the next world. Forgiveness alone will not remove them, nor will dying.

50 Your grace-filled soul *matters*. Only when you embrace love, joy and peace will you come to fulfillment.

51 Even though Mommy is perfectly willing to forgive her child for everything, her forgiveness is meaningless if the *child* does not learn and mature.

52 The life you live matters.

53 The grace of existence is the essence of your nature.

54 Grace is love.

55 Grace is life.

56 Grace is oneness.

57 Grace is truth.

58 Truth is the only religion.

---

[1] NT First Corinthians 13:12

Chapter 6
Divinity's Children

1 Saint Paul writes in the New Testament, "For by grace you have been saved through faith, and that not of yourselves: it is the gift of God."[1]

2 The Future Testament would like to offer a new translation:

> There is nothing you can do,
> no act, no ability or performance,
> that can make you any more
> or less loved in the eyes of God.

3 Humans everywhere reach for meaning and value.

4 Sadly, the vast majority of people find their meaning in the jobs they do, the prestige they have and the money they earn. But these, too, are forms of ritualized, externalized grace.

5 Having lost our sense of self-worth, unable to connect to God or to the eternity that surrounds us, unable to find the grace which is ours simply by being alive, we substitute our intrinsic value with an artificial one.

6 We substitute a material worth we *have* for the intrinsic worth that we *are* as Yahweh's children.

7 We get degrees and pretend to *know* something. We earn money and imagine we are *worth* something.

8 We accomplish something in the *outer* world and suppose that that we have improved our *inner* world.

9 This is youthful thinking, entirely understandable but misguided.

10 A loving mother does not love her child more because he accomplishes something.

11 A child who learns quickly is not more lovable than if she struggles.

12 A loving parent only rejoices for the sake of her child, that she has done something that will help the child grow. But the child is no more *lovable*, no more *valuable*, no more *important* and no more *loved* than before.

---

[1] NT Ephesians 2:8

13 Like Esau,[1] we sell our birthright as Divinity's Children for external acclaim.

14 Then we imagine people who have not achieved *our* external accomplishments are less worthy than ourselves.

15 Meanwhile, the truth of God is Love: love *of* all, *in* all, *for* all.

16 True grace realizes there is nothing we can *do* to be any more or any less loved by Yahweh.

17 Yes, the life you live does matter, but love is never a matter of performance.

18 The grace of your existence expresses itself as your unique talents.

19 The extent to which you use your grace to help others is the extent to which you grow toward your ultimate fulfillment.

20 That is the heart of grace, unfolding in our world.

21 Love, life and liberty forever remain gifts of grace, expressions of our oneness with the Creator.

22 The Greek word that has been translated in our Bibles as grace is "karis." Karis could just as correctly be translated as *joy, exuberance,* the excited *lust for life.*

23 Grace is joy.

24 Joy is the fruit of the Spirit.

25 The Spirit is life.

26 Grace is life.

27 Instead of *living* grace, we have dogmatized it, making grace something we *get* because God watched Jesus bleed and die.

28 Grace longs to renew our hearts:

Grace is life,
life is joy,
joy is the fruit of the Spirit,
the fruit of the Spirit is
the fruition of your soul,
the fruition of your soul is salvation,
and salvation is
you, the anointed one,
Christ in the flesh.

29 That is the truth of grace.

30 Grace is joy.

31 Grace is life.

---

[1] OT Genesis 25:29 - 34

32 Grace is life worth living.

33 Like the people of Old Testament times, we have found that the life we live *does* matter, but it's not a question of seeking favor so that everything goes well.

34 Like the people of New Testament times, we see that there *is* an afterlife, but heaven cannot be purchased at someone else's expense.

35 But what are we to do, what are we supposed to think, when grace cannot be found? When calamity strikes, when we are desperately fearful, what then?

36 If the Book of Grace is true, what do we do with the mountains of evidence to the contrary?

37 Starving children, genocidal wars, calamities, holocausts, birth defects, innocents dying for lack of care… how should we respond when Yahweh's world of grace appears to be a cesspool of suffering and misery?

38 Let us turn to the Book of Pain.

The Future Testament

Book Ten: The Book of Pain

Chapter 1
The Grace of Pain

1 Our notions about pain are too large.

2 From our infancy, every little irritation makes us scream.

3 The smallest inconvenience, the tiniest physical or emotional pain, can cause us to cry aloud or shriek in our souls about the injustice of the Universe.

4 For many people, the simple existence of pain makes it impossible to conceive of God.

5 Why would a loving God allow the pain and misery we see on the planet?

6 If God is love, why is there suffering? Why are there birth defects?

7 How could a loving "god" allow sudden infant death syndrome?

8 Why is there cancer? What about hurricanes, earthquakes, tsunamis, volcanoes, forest fires…

9 If God is love, we scream, what is natural about natural disasters?

10 To many, the misery on this planet is proof enough that, if there is a God, He is despotic and evil, not to be worshiped.

11 The Future Testament hopes to address these sentiments.

12 Learn this deeply: Ultimately, pain is grace.

13 People will ignore history and repeat its mistakes. We will ignore our intuition, even when we know it is right.

14 We will ignore the messages of our elders; we will ignore the warning signs in our traffic systems.

15 We will ignore the scriptures, the saints, the prophets, the Messiah, our pastors, priests and popes.

16 There is *only one thing* we will not ignore: our pain.

17 Pain is our greatest teacher.

18 We can't ignore our pain.

19 Pain is a warning, telling us that something is wrong.

20 Regrettably, some children are born with a neural condition that makes it impossible for them to feel pain at all. These children are in the gravest danger because they can put their hands in burning flames and experience no discomfort. Because they are completely disconnected from normal pain sensors, such children have to be taught other warning mechanisms.

21 Pain exists to teach us, to warn us, to let us know that something is out of balance, disconnected.

22 Pain lets us know something is wrong.

23 Pain exists on many levels, and its warnings apply to all the realms that compose our being.

> The physical *body* has pain sensors
> to protect it from harm.
> Our *hearts* are meant to cry in anguish
> at the suffering we see around us.
> Our *minds* are meant to recoil in horror
> in the face of disaster.
> Our *spirits* are meant to groan
> as we encounter our lost world,
> out of balance with each other, nature and God.

Chapter 2
Pain the Teacher

1 Pain is here to teach, inform and guide. Learn from it.

2 Pain can bring our attention to an issue that desperately needs our care.

3 Pain can help us focus on areas that we can heal.

4 But often, though we can learn from pain, we do not.

5 When we fail to learn from our own pain, we disregard one of the greatest teachers we have.

6 To be very clear, there are only three ways to learn:

> Learn through your own experiences,
> learn from someone else's experiences, or
> do not learn at all.

7 There is no other option.

8 Pain is meant to be an impetus for healing.

9 Pain is meant to be a guidepost for the present and a teaching mechanism for the future.

10 The knowledge that a plant, insect or animal is poisonous comes from someone being poisoned.

11 Harmful chemicals were not known to be harmful until someone was harmed.

12 As our lives experience those things that bring us pain, we are meant to learn the lessons of our pain and to teach future generations how to avoid the same pitfalls.

13 The Universe is so incomprehensibly vast, and life is so short, that we can learn very little directly.

14 Each one of us plays but one tiny note in the symphony of eternity, and no one has enough time, energy or potential to discover it all.

15 Literacy for the entire world must be championed so that we can hear the whole symphony.

16 Reading, writing and learning from the past will redeem the suffering that has gone before.

17 Literacy will assist us in our present lives and help guide us into the glorious future that is our true destiny.

18 We redeem our pain through the teaching we pass along to the next generation.

19 Pain is the greatest teacher, for pain alone we will never ignore.

20 Our notions of suffering and pain form a matrix of four scenarios:

21 Evil people prosper, and we are outraged.

22 Evil people suffer, and we are satisfied by vengeance.

23 Good people suffer, and we rant about the injustice of the Universe.

24 Good people gain, and we wonder why the other three conditions even have to exist.

25 This suffering matrix shows us that our views of pain are too large.

26 A person may have lived a life of happiness, goodness and love, but the one thing they will recount as their life's story is trauma and tragedy.

At the end of what is essentially a wonderful day,
when the manifold systems that are involved in your life,
from the miracles of your body
to the glories of the biosphere,
to the complexities of society,
to the technologies we have invented,
every bit of it working in perfect harmony...

what we will most often focus on,
remember, discuss
and immortalize in our journals
is the *one tiny thing* that went wrong.

27 In a world where, by the billions, people live lives of happiness and progress, we focus almost exclusively on suffering.

28 Our notions of pain are too large.

29 Pain must not be ignored or avoided. But if we are to become all that God has for us in our fulfillment, as Christ is formed in us, we must balance our ideas about pain.

30 We must learn to put pain in its proper place: neither ignore it or minimize it, nor make it the focus of our lives. We need to acknowledge pain as our teacher and learn from it.

31 No mother would ever define her infant child on the basis of what she found in the child's diaper. Yet that kind of thinking is how we approach life, defining our existence of the basis of the occasional mess we have to clean up.

32 The ways in which we *treat* and *resolve* our pain are inadequate: our ways are too small.

33 We make too much of our pain because we have made the *resolutions* of pain too small.

34 Our compensations for pain are often misguided.

35 We will suffer, but we will not share what we have learned with others.

36 In silence, we mistakenly congratulate ourselves for suffering.

37 Frequently, thinking there is no lesson to be learned from our suffering, we will learn nothing at all.

38 Pain is our educator, but we ignore the curriculum.

39 We treat *symptoms* while ignoring *cause*.

40 Pain can be a symptom of a problem that is not immediately apparent, like a neck that throbs because of a back injury.

41 A child may die of starvation due to greed on the other side of the planet.

42 This is a *Uni*-verse. As all the parts of our body are interconnected, so all people in the Universe are interconnected.

43 By failing to heed the lessons that pain should teach us, we avoid healing our disconnected souls.

44 As we reestablish our interconnectedness, we will learn to avoid

painful situations, from personal to national to global.[1]

45 The mega-wealth of the few and the infernal poverty of the many can only exist simultaneously in fractured humanity.

46 We are one: there is a direct connection between one person's wealth and another person's poverty, one's exultation and another's pain.

47 Wall Street, Main Street and a village's dirt path are all on the *same* street.

48 Resolve the causative back injury, and the neck will be healed as well.

49 Heal the cause and the symptoms vanish.

50 As the hearts of the selfish begin to be enlightened by the love of their indwelling spirit, the physical suffering of the masses will end.

Chapter 3
The Pitfalls of Avoidance

1 Pain is the experience; suffering is how we *react* to it.

2 Pain, while discomforting, need not become all-consuming suffering.

3 While on the cross, Jesus experienced great pain. However, the pain did not consume his consciousness.

4 When we take a more mature attitude toward pain, allowing past hurts to become present lessons, we can turn our discomfort (whether physical, emotional, mental or spiritual) into the wisdom of future generations.

5 In that way, we *redeem* pain.

6 Most of us make more of pain than we should.

7 We will often do everything possible to avoid even the slightest pain. We avoid pain with chemicals, isolation, depression, apathy and narcissism.

8 We will use a wide variety of *drugs*, from aspirin to heroin, ecstasy to alcohol.

9 We medicate ourselves chemically so that we are numbed to whatever pain we might experience.

10 The difficulty with chemical avoidance is that we become dependent on *external* agents to perform an *internal* function.

---

[1] FT Eternity 1:22 - 28

11 The extent to which we rely upon *any* external agent is the extent to which we lose nature's wisdom. We lose the natural abilities we replace with unnatural means; we lose control.

12 Sit in a wheelchair long enough and you will lose the ability to walk. Use a calculator long enough and you will be unable to add. Use spell-checking long enough and you cannot spell.

13 Rely on someone else's judgment, and you lose your ability to decide.

14 Misuse of chemicals results in weakening our organic defenses to the point they no longer function.

15 Worse, a constant regime of drugs to *avoid* pain makes it impossible to *feel* pain.

16 Painkillers kill the teacher.

17 If you are always numbed with a blanket of chemical comfort, how will you know when your system is in danger?

18 People hurt themselves while they are self-medicating precisely because they don't experience pain. The body's natural warning system is shut down.

19 Our society has shown us that the preventative avoidance of pain through chemicals is a dangerous thing to do.

20 However, chemical lessening of pain for a person who has a real problem is quite different.

21 In the case of true need, treatment of pain, by whatever means, is compassion and mercy.

22 We are out of balance. Pain suppressors are over-prescribed for healthy people, but we withhold treatment from the genuinely needy.

23 We need the simple balance of connecting knowledge with wisdom, two of the primary roots on the Tree of Life.

24 People who are in genuine pain need comfort, as a bridge to healing the *cause* of pain.

25 If the patient has a broken leg, no other cause for the pain need be explored. Allowing the patient's pain to continue to the point of torture is unnecessarily cruel.

26 For healthy people to be numbed with physical or psychotropic medications is likewise very dangerous.

27 It is also dangerous to avoid pain through *isolation*.

28 Isolation can be as dangerous as drugs.

29 You may think that if you don't come into contact with illness, you won't get sick. But our bodies have a miraculous immune system that *requires* exposure to illness.

30 From a child's birth, the immune system must be allowed to encounter bacteria and viruses to build resistance and strengthen overall health.

31 Failure to develop the immune system leaves us with no natural defenses.

32 The immune system, just like muscles, needs to be exercised to be strong.

33 Well-intended parents who isolate their children from every possible contagion are ultimately subjecting their children to life-threatening circumstances.

34 A small head cold can quickly become deadly when the immune system is weak or has not been strengthened normally.

35 Likewise, you may think that if you avoid evil, it cannot hurt you. But the soul has its own miraculous immune system that *requires* contact with evil.

36 Like the child prevented from developing a strong immune system, souls that avoid all discomfort become vulnerable, at risk of great damage.

37 When we isolate ourselves from the world, living without the risk of human interaction, we become emotionally weakened, empty and vacant.

38 We also avoid pain through self-indulgent *depression*, losing faith that life is worth living.

39 We allow our problems to possess our lives and ignore the multitude of blessings around us.

40 *Apathy* likewise improperly avoids pain. We become dead inside.

41 We stop caring about the conditions of others and are apathetic to the genuine suffering of people around us.

42 Apathy is a form of isolationism that leads to the destruction of everything human, for the hallmark of humanity is, as Saint Paul says, "Now abide faith, hope and love; but the greatest of these is love."[1]

43 When we have lost our hope, we are in depression.

44 When we have lost our love, we are in apathy, oblivious to all around us, caring only for ourselves.

45 Apathy leads to the death of soul.

46 We also avoid pain with *narcissism*. Narcissism is related to isolationism and apathy, where we only care about ourselves.

---

[1]NT First Corinthians 13:13

47 The narcissist's solution to problems is self-indulgence and isolation, accompanied by massive doses of apathy.

48 Narcissism is the very heart of the materialistic, commercial, consumerist code of life on the planet today.

49 Narcissism wants you to avoid everything that doesn't feel good. It is its own type of drug.

50 Narcissism is deadening because it limits love to only one thing: the ego.

51 But, most damaging to the soul, the narcissist's code says that you should always be happy.

52 Narcissism only chooses what is *pleasant*, regardless of what is *right*.

53 Jesus wept.

54 Apathy, avoidance, narcissism: these are not to be confused with genuine suffering.

55 As people who are in real pain need comfort, people who experience tragedy need compassion that allows them to mourn and heal at their own pace.

56 Grief is personal and must be allowed to be expressed in freedom, without expectations.

57 Be not deceived: the true path to growth involves pain.

58 Even Jesus, our brother, model and destiny, felt pain. He felt sorrow. He was *not* always happy.

59 He loved, healed, inspired and served; his earthly reward was execution.

60 The love we share as children of God is unlimited. It is only by connecting with others that we find who and what we really are.

61 True love is often inconvenient, uncomfortable, even painful.

62 The wisdom of the heart needs to be in balance with the knowledge of the mind.

63 The human race cannot be fulfilled by people who are pursuing only what is *pleasant*; the human race will be fulfilled pursuing what is *right*.

64 Doing right by struggling against the injustices of the world will lead to the fulfillment of humanity.

65 Doing right by caring for the suffering and the starving will lead to the kingdom of God.

Chapter 4
The Pitfalls of Vengeance

1 When we are hurt, we want to hurt someone else in return.

2 Vengeance is one of the greatest challenges facing the human race.

3 How do we deal with those who have wronged us or society? What do we do with criminals? What do we do with people who physically or emotionally abuse? How do we fight evil, without *becoming* the very evil we are opposing?

4 Every person who commits an act of violence feels, on some level, they are justified because of a previous hurt.

5 From the beginning of time, all the way back to Cain and Abel, this is our rallying cry: "The other guy started it."

6 Vengeance is the primary way the human race has tried to solve its problems for all of history.

7 Sometimes we do not hurt the one who specifically hurt us, but we find someone else to pass our anger to.

8 Some people take the hurt out upon themselves, assuming blame and internalizing more hurt than the original problem.

9 Our desire for vengeance assures that all hurts continue to reverberate around the globe, throughout all the generations.

10 The truth is that God asks for none of this.

11 The true pathway is not to blame yourself, pass the pain along, nor escalate it.

12 The true pathway asks us to become the anointed one. We're asked to become the Messiah, the Christ, for that is our true destiny and fulfillment.

13 We are all invited to become the lamb of God, to help *absorb* the pains of the world, as Jesus demonstrated.

14 When someone hurts us, we are invited to become the Messiah, absorb the pain, and allow it to disappear.

15 Christ, having died once, need never die again. "It is finished,"[1] he said.

16 Pain need not reverberate to the next person.

17 Pain need not escalate into war.

---

[1] NT John 19:30

18 The hurt can die away if someone is willing to absorb the pain through forgiveness.

19 In becoming the gentle lamb, we provide those who wrong us the opportunity to see what God showed the world in Jesus the Christ.

20 Forgiveness is the only pathway to peace.

21 Annihilation, from technologies uncontrollable by our infantile morality, is the only alternative destiny.

Chapter 5
Two Types of Forgiveness

1 The first Christ asked God to forgive people because they did *not* know what they were doing.

2 The Christ reborn in all of us has a much harder job: we must ask God to forgive people because they *do* know what they are doing.

3 It is essential to know that there are *two* types of forgiveness.

4 The first type of forgiveness is unilateral and unconditional; the second is bilateral and conditional.

5 Jesus demonstrated unconditional forgiveness as the lamb: "Father, forgive them for they know not what they do."[1]

6 If someone has wronged you, you are invited to embrace this first kind of forgiveness and, without any requirements, decide to completely forgive the person who has wronged you.

7 Unconditional forgiveness is given not for the sake of the other, but for yourself.

8 Unconditional forgiveness liberates *you*.

9 It is for your own sake that you grant unconditional forgiveness. You are then free to live without spending any time in vengeance, hatred, sorrow, remorse or negative repercussions of any kind.

10 Unilateral forgiveness allows you to be well and truly free. It is a vital component of your liberty.

11 However, unilateral forgiveness does *not* mean that you must continue a relationship with those who do wrong.

12 The second kind of forgiveness restores the relationship, but it is *conditional*.[2]

---

[1] NT Luke 23:34
[2] NT Luke 17:3

13 Wisdom requires you to create boundaries for those who you know would harm you or your children.

14 The person who has granted the unilateral forgiveness of the lamb is free from the pains of vengeance, but that *does not mean* that he needs to allow himself to be victimized again.

15 This is why the scripture makes it clear that Christ, having died once, need never die again.[1] If someone wrongs you, you are under no obligation to put yourself in a position where they can continue.

16 Indeed, the entire relationship may be lost, based upon the severity of the offense.

17 It may even be necessary for you to engage the justice system, to assure that this person cannot harm another.

18 The scripture says that those who do wrong must come to *repentance*, which is a new way of thinking. Additionally, they must *recognize* their fault, experience *remorse*, *resolve* to live according to their new ways, and do everything they can to *repair* the damage, if possible.

19 This is the basis of many twelve-step programs of healing.

20 If the wrongdoer genuinely repents, we are then required to restore the relationship, offering the second kind of forgiveness, a forgiveness of relational restoration based upon the wrongdoer's repentance, recognition, remorse, resolve and repair.

21 The human race could not exist if every wrong led to the loss of relationship. There would be no hope.

22 But the other extreme would also destroy life, if every wrong would be allowed to continue without consequence.

23 There's beautiful wisdom in Yahweh's two-fold system of forgiveness.

24 When you truly understand both kinds of forgiveness, heart and mind are joined, and the ability to form healthy boundaries with those who have hurt you is established in loving discernment.

25 Those who are able to forgive unconditionally spend their lives free from re-living hurts and pain, free from victimhood, free to keep old relationships and free to form new ones.

26 Genuine repentance enables you to re-establish relationships with those you have wronged.

27 These ideas are difficult for the human race to both comprehend and act upon.

---

[1] NT Romans 6:9

28 Dealing with wrongdoers is one of the greatest challenges facing humanity. How do we fight injustice without being unjust? How do we stop murder without killing? How do we oppose terrorism without becoming terrorists?

29 On the individual, corporate, national and global scale, the notion of vengeance has only led to more vengeance.

30 The way of the lamb of God, the Christ, offers a different vision.

31 Ultimately, the purpose of all our pain is to give us hope.

Chapter 6
Love and Pain

1 Pain is grace.

2 Pain is a gift from God, letting us know that something is wrong.

3 God adds to this gift by providing the opportunity to discover the causes of our pain and offering us the ability to serve the world by passing our wisdom along to future generations.

4 The question is nearly universal: "If God is good, loving and powerful, why does suffering exist?" The Future Testament would like to submit that asking "why" is misguided.

5 From the New Testament:

> As he [Jesus] went along, he saw a man blind from birth.
> His disciples asked him, "Rabbi, who sinned,
> this man or his parents, that he was born blind?"
> "Neither this man nor his parents sinned," said Jesus,
> "but this happened so that the work of God
> might be displayed in his life."[1]

6 Jesus' response tells the disciples to *not ask why*. "Why" is irrelevant.

7 Sometimes the reasons "why" lie beyond or beneath human comprehension.

8 Sometimes the reason why hundreds of thousands of people die in an earthquake is simply because two tectonic plates that have been building up pressure for millions of years suddenly move and release pressure.

9 The reason "why" is nothing more or less than that.

10 An earthquake lacks a moral component.

---

[1] NT John 9:1 - 3

11 Sometimes a birth defect is nothing more or less than one microscopic chemical in a DNA strand failing to make a connection. There is no moral reason for it.

12 Natural disasters, personal or global, are not Yahweh's punishment.

13 The question "why?" is well intended, but misguided.

14 The story of the blind man tells us what really matters: we need to work for healing!

15 Each situation is an opportunity to work for what is right. The "why" is of no consequence.

16 Whenever tragedy occurs, we have the ability to turn darkness into light.

17 A huge calamity gives us the opportunity to transform our armies of war into armies of healing and service, feeding the desperate and comforting the homeless.

18 Imagine a world where armies are dispatched around the globe, not to kill, but to heal.

19 We can have faith and hope that it can happen; with enough love, it *will* happen.

20 Tragedies invite us to beat our swords into plowshares[1] and work for the peace we seek.

21 With every pain comes an opportunity, as we respond with love.

22 From personal to global levels, we can use tragedy as an opportunity to heal, restore, learn and grow.

23 A little boy falls off his bike and breaks his arm; he gets cleaned up, the arm is set in a cast, and the break heals. Loving parents will make certain he also learns a valuable lesson about caution. The lesson will serve him for the remainder of his life and the lives of his children.

24 Do not trouble yourself seeking some moral cause for suffering.

25 Rather, see suffering as an opportunity to transform bad into good, wrong into right and darkness into light.

26 Your life is meant to reflect Jesus' life; you are invited to be the light of the world,[2] doing what is right, transforming suffering into love at every opportunity.

27 God does not cause our suffering, but works to heal it.

28 The proclamation of the scripture is that, though God does not cause harm, God is the force that works to heal.

---

[1] OT Isaiah 2:4
[2] NT Matthew 5:14

29 As Saint Paul says, "For I am convinced that all things work together for good, for those who love God and are called according to His purpose."[1]

30 For our part, we are called to love Him and to be open vessels of His love and grace. Yahweh's purpose is to expand the light of love, and we are called to be vessels for that sharing.

31 The essence of faith is assurance. When we lose hope, we've lost our confidence that things will get better, and we often lose ourselves in despair.

32 But with hope comes the gift of assurance that, no matter how horrible the situation, we can work to make it better.

33 We can use what we have learned to improve the future of the human race.

34 Our thoughts of pain are too large. If we will look at our pain through the lens of faith, we will see our pain in the perspective that leads to learning and growth. We will see our pain from Yahweh's perspective.

35 Think about your past problems. At the time, those problems loomed large and frightening, but now they look quite different. Problems in retrospect look smaller, less significant, less frightening, even humorous.

36 Applying past experience to present reality, when you encounter a problem, have faith to know in advance that healing will come.

37 All tears shall pass away.[2]

38 Your future deliverance can become your present reality.

39 The lens of faith is one of our greatest gifts, if we will use it.

40 The gift of faith warps time, allowing us to receive, here and now, the benefits of resolutions that lie in the future.

---

[1] NT Romans 8:28
[2] NT Revelation 21:4

Chapter 7
Glory to Be Revealed

1 Memorize this essential verse from the New Testament:

"I consider that our present sufferings
are not worth comparing with the
glory that will be revealed in us."[1]

2 If you could embrace only one verse in the core of your being, this verse, by itself, would transform you.

3 If it were to be embraced by all, the planet would be returned to paradise almost overnight.

4 Our current sufferings will lead to magnificent renewal.

5 The struggles of learning cannot be compared to the glories of knowledge.

6 The pain of war cannot be compared to a universal season of peace.

7 Even a life filled with suffering cannot be compared to the glory to be discovered in eternity.

8 Notice, once again, how the notions in the Future Testament are connected:

Pain can lead to a fulfilling rebirth,
your liberty as *Christ in the flesh.*
But in order to become the Christ, you
must be able to deal with your *pain.*
You must be able to see *pain* as a gift of *grace.*
Then, with a heart of *faith,* you can find your *fulfillment.*

9 Pain is temporary.

10 Pain comes to an end.

11 Pain stops.

12 This is the real meaning of "the wages of sin is death."[2] Whenever our soul wanders into realms of sin and darkness, those detours must die (stop), returning us to the pristine goodness that is our birthright.

13 Jesus' pain on the cross stopped.

14 The torture of the Holocaust came to an end.

---

[1] NT Romans 8:18
[2] NT Romans 6:23

15 Even the horror of Jesus' crucifixion and the abomination of the Holocaust cannot be compared to eternities of infinite souls radiating boundless love, joy and peace.

16 Regardless of the pain of the entire world, our present sufferings cannot be compared to the glory that is about to be revealed *in* us, *through* us, *as* us.

17 In conclusion, pain is grace. Learn this well.

18 But be careful to avoid the shortcuts and substitutes: no person can bear another's pain. We can learn, and we can teach, but each person must learn their own lessons.

19 Meditate upon the parable of the butterfly:

> The caterpillar enters a cocoon of its own making
> and miraculously transforms into a butterfly.
> The butterfly then uses its infant strength to break the cocoon.
> If you do the butterfly the "favor" of removing the cocoon,
> thinking you are helping to free it from bondage,
> the butterfly will lay undeveloped and will die.
> It is only the process of fighting to escape its self-made cocoon
> that will push the life-giving enzymes to the ends of its wings
> and give the butterfly the strength necessary
> to arise like Christ from the tomb.

20 Only your own ego-death, upon your unique cross, can lead to your own resurrection.

21 In a cosmos of eternal life, even the greatest disasters are but a detour.

22 Jesus' crucifixion lasted hours, but his resurrection lasts forever.

23 Every temporal pain sprouts seeds of eternal glory that simply cannot be compared to the pain.

24 "A woman giving birth to a child has pain because her time has come; but when her baby is born she forgets the anguish because of her joy that a child is born into the world."[1]

25 Goodness, hope and love rise from the ashes of misery.

26 When we feel pain, we learn compassion.

27 When we feel another's hate, we learn love.

28 When we feel the emptiness of imprisonment, we learn to cherish liberty.

29 When we are sick with disease, we learn to value health.

30 When we feel another's scorn, we learn to forgive.

---

[1] NT John 16:21

This is forever the mystery,
the eternal redemption,
of dark into light,
of cold death into warm rebirth,
of wrong into right,
of bad into good,
of pain into the love of God.
Elsewise, there could be no life at all.

The Future Testament

Book Eleven: The Book of God

Chapter 1
The Changeless Core

1 Our notions about God are too small. They always will be, and it cannot be any other way.

2 Beyond infinite, God is an infinite number of infinities, multiplied together.

3 With every treasure we uncover there yet remains an ocean of undiscovered splendor just beyond our reach.

4 When the Future Testament was written, the largest known prime number was written with 13 million digits; and we know, as a certain fact, there are an *infinite* number of primes larger than that one.

5 The purpose of our learning is to forever increase the height of the tower upon which we stand, to better survey the immeasurable horizons of our unknowing.

6 This is as it always shall be, for the pursuit of God is vast and unbounded.

7 And the quest for God is the pursuit of ourselves.

8 Our known Universe contains hundreds of billions of galaxies, each containing billions of stars; only God Himself, literally, knows how many of those solar systems contain inhabitable planets.

9 But the promise of fulfillment is this: in the end, at the limit of all eternities, we will fully know God, as God fully knows us.[1] At that time we will *be* the Mind of God, knowing ourselves.[2]

10 Let the pursuit of science be the quest for the Divine.

11 In our youth, it was easy to think of things as separate. We put religion in one department, math in another, sociology, biology, chemistry and physics all in their own departments.

12 We are learning daily that each of these is actually a reflection of the other, that they are astoundingly connected in ways that were unimaginable even a few years ago.

---

[1] NT First Corinthians 13:12
[2] NT First Corinthians 2:11

13 As we seek for God, we use the world around us to make comparisons, correlations and analogies.

14 God is ineffable. This is why the world's religious writings are full of parables and poetry.

15 Let the Universe be your parable of God.

16 Yahweh is everything we see, and the power by which we see.

17 God is everything that we know, and the power by which we know.

18 God is everything we hear, and the mystery that enables us to hear.

19 So we look around us, gazing into the heavens and peering into the atom, to find clues about the transcendent majesty that is God, the One who becomes One.

20 But ultimately, we are looking even deeper than that.

21 When we contemplate Divinity, we are looking for that which remains permanent in a sea of change, what remains eternal in a world of cultural mutability.

22 Seeking Yahweh's word in scripture, we desire to know eternal truth, apart from the social norms of the times. Indeed, such perceptions have created all the world's religions and denominations.

23 Obviously, much has changed in our understanding over the centuries.

24 We know infinitely more about the physical Universe than Moses or Jesus could have ever imagined.

25 We have learned much about the size of the Universe and the structure of matter, down to sub-sub-atomic particles.

26 We have learned about the nature of the cell, and we can modify DNA in a laboratory.

27 And yet, that which underlies the Universe from macro to micro remains constant: God.

28 God is love, and forever will be. Love may change form, but love *is*, and will always *be*.

29 God is light, and forever will be.

30 It is said that when the student is ready, the teacher appears.

31 From time immemorial, humanity has sought to know God, but we can only understand God through what we know at the time.

32 When we are children, our understanding of God is childlike.

33 When we mature, our greater range of knowledge allows us to know God in broader terms.

34 Although many understandings have changed, the core conception of God as love remains forever true.

35 Light, life and law are love made manifest.

Chapter 2
Father God and Mother Nature

1 In the days of old, the people of Sinai received a new revelation: God is our Father, a loving guide in our growth, occasionally cruel but only in order to protect us from harm.

2 The notion of God as parent remains one of the key parables that we use, today and forever, to learn the nature of God.

3 Unfortunately, because many humans have less than ideal earthly parents as role models, our notions of God suffer.

4 Nevertheless, most of us know that truly loving parents do not condemn their children.

5 Loving parents care only that their children grow, learn and reach their full potential.

6 The human race has come to think of God as father and the Earth as mother. As the source of all, God has no gender, for both male and female spring from the same source.

7 However, the ideas of masculinity and femininity provide a fertile ground for understanding the source.

8 The male is the seed giver, the impetus; the female is the life-giver, providing form to the seed.

9 The male is pure potential; the female is dynamic, acting upon that potential.

10 The father–male principle is invisible; the mother–female principle gives form to the invisible.

11 Father God and Mother Nature are forever the twin poles between which the sacred dance of creation moves.

12 Since the Earth does indeed declare Yahweh's handiwork,[1] the love of parent for child is the greatest parable we have for the true nature of the Divine.

13 Always remember: it is impossible for you to love your children more than God loves you.

14 This one idea can heal the hearts of Yahweh's children and help transform the planet.

15 God only wants His beloved children to grow to their full potential: Christ, the anointing of God, the fruit of the Spirit, the fruition of your existence.

---

[1] OT Psalm 19

16 The fallen notions of God as some capricious, vindictive monster who would kill his son to placate himself for our shortcomings is simply impossible for a loving father.

17 Genesis proclaims that we are made in Yahweh's image;[1] therefore, all of Yahweh's nature and attributes exist within us.

18 Astonishingly, God's sacred name "Yahweh,"[2] spelled vertically in the ancient Hebrew letters, forms a pictogram of a human being.

19 You are created in the image and likeness of Yahweh's holy Name, a visual representation of God in fleshly form.

20 Indeed, you are God's Name.

21 From the beginning, the Old Testament has been a sacred testimonial to the intimate relationship between God and humanity.

22 Learn well the meaning, the power and the revelation of Yahweh's sacred Name.

23 For centuries, Jesus has acted as elder brother and guide, helping the human race to move forward in our quest for divinity.

24 The Future Testament wants to take the human race a step further, focusing on the fact that every one of us is called to be Christ, God in the flesh.

25 Our fulfillment and indeed, the purpose of our lives, is when Christ is formed in us.

26 Be not confused: Jesus made it quite plain that we are one common family. Jesus said he was going to *his* father and to *our* father, to *his* God and to *our* God.[3]

27 As he is, we will be.[4]

28 From God as distant father (Old Testament), to God incarnate in one person (New Testament), to God incarnate in every person (Future Testament), there is an obvious progression.

29 God is now inviting us to celebrate *every* human being as Christ in the flesh.

---

[1] OT Genesis 1:26
[2] OT Exodus 3:14
[3] NT John 20:17
[4] NT First John 3:2 & 3

30 The birthday of every human being should be celebrated as Christmas.

31 "Joy to the world, the Lord has come!" Let this ecstasy be proclaimed of every boy and girl born!

32 Each child is God in the flesh, incarnate love sent to heal the world.

Chapter 3
The New World

1 Since Jesus left the Earth, mankind has worked diligently to learn as much as we can about Yahweh's physical Universe.

2 We have discovered much.

3 Before time began...bubbling off of the face of no-thing-ness...out of the necessity of self-existence...the pure Spirit of God willed to have consciousness, life and body.

4 We now know, through the laws of conservation, that nothing is ever created or destroyed. Things only change form; "creation" is an illusion, a misnomer.

5 The Universe has *not* been shaped in the way a potter molds clay into vessels; rather, the Universe has been *growing* from Yahweh's own being, like a snail growing its own shell or like a caterpillar growing its own cocoon.

6 We know that we are made up of the very stuff of God.

7 God's blood pumps in our veins.

8 We are blood cells in God's body.

9 The laws of conservation explain why "as above, so below" is always true; things change form, but their essence remains constant.

10 We can learn from everything because everything is within God.

11 And as we learn everything about everything, we learn about God and about ourselves, Yahweh's reflections in the world.

12 Jesus taught in parables, simple stories using what the people knew to illustrate the nature of God.

13 Knowledge has increased exponentially, and our advances in science, mathematics and language can create for us an infinite variety of modern parables.

14 Learn everything about everything; it will lead you to fulfillment.

15 Learn the parable of the Universe: energy and mass are a continuum, and all energy/mass in the Universe is Yahweh's body.

16 Though mind-numbing and impossibly vast, the Universe is only Yahweh's *physical* body; God's heart and mind lie beyond the reaches of the physical Universe.

17 Learn the parable of fractals, wherein everything to be known about an entire system can be seen in every tiny part.

18 Learn the parable of the Mandelbrot set. It has always been here, waiting to be discovered, since the beginning of time. Learn how the large Mandelbrot set is one without a second, and contains within it infinite numbers of "minibrots," each of which reflects the fullness of the large Mandelbrot.

19 Learn the parable of relativity: $e = mc^2$.

20 Learn the parable of light. God is light.[1]

21 Learn the parable of the ocean. Though it is vast and infinite, individual molecules of water break off through evaporation, only to return to the ocean and reclaim their totality.

22 God is a vast ocean from which we bubble, and as we are called to return to God, we reclaim the divinity that has been ours from the beginning.

23 The life cycle that can be seen in oceans and fractals is clearly shown in the New Testament through Jesus' life:

"Your attitude should be the same as that of Christ Jesus: who, being in very nature God, did not consider equality with God something to be grasped, but made himself nothing, taking the very nature of a servant, being made in human likeness. And being found in appearance as a man, he humbled himself and became obedient to death – even death on a cross. Therefore God exalted him to the highest place."[2]

24 This is the Breath of God:

God dies, so we can live, so
we can die, so God can live.

25 This same four-fold process reflects itself throughout all of nature.

26 Learn the parable of the child:

Unconscious unity turns to unconscious separation,
then conscious separation, and ultimately conscious unity.
The baby begins in the womb,
unconsciously connected with the mother.
At birth, the baby becomes disconnected,

---

[1] NT First John 1:5
[2] NT Philippians 2:5 - 9

though unconscious of the fact.
Through the process of self-awareness,
the child becomes consciously separate.
This is the ego state,
Adam and Eve in the fall,
where humanity finds itself today.
Then, through the divinity of love,
the maturing soul is called to consciously
re-connect and re-unite.

27 This explains the New Testament scripture, "In God we live and move and have our being."[1]

28 All of us are living the four-fold parable of the child as we progress to God-consciousness.

29 Learn the parable of the blood cell:

Every cell has a personal structure,
including cell walls separating it from all other cells.
While each cell has its individual purpose,
every cell contains within it the DNA that
associates it with every other cell in the body.
Yet each cell shares the duty to perform
its function in relationship with all the cells around it,
in service to the one body whose abilities are
far beyond the scope of any individual cell.

30 We, humanity as a whole, are being formed into the body of Christ.[2]

31 We are, every one of us, a living cell in the body of Christ, with individual functions and identities, and yet we share the same Christ-DNA with the whole of humanity.

32 We are being built up into one super-conscious being, the likes of which we cannot begin to imagine.

33 Learn the parable of the mainframe computer: dumb terminals become autonomous personal computers, which eventually become linked to create a super-computer incalculably greater than any mainframe could have been.

34 That is the Breath of God, the body of Christ.

35 The Breath of God is a system, a cycle, a process; it is being extended throughout the Universe for eternity.

---

[1] NT Acts 17:28
[2] NT First Corinthians 12:27

36 Learn the parable of the car: you relate to your automobile in exactly the same way your soul relates to your body.

37 Death is not the end. It is a beginning, no more significant than exiting your car.

38 Your body, though glorious and wondrous, is only the vehicle that carries your soul.

39 Your consciousness, thoughts, feelings, hopes, dreams, memories and desires will live on, for you are an eternal spiritual being temporarily housed in a biological shell.

40 Learn the parable of Gödel's Incompleteness Theorem, which tells us that there will always be truths we *know* are true but that we cannot *prove*.

41 Our quest for God is constant and eternal; it will never stop and will forever grow.

42 Each new answer leads to a hundred new questions, and the mystery will forever keep us moving forward.

43 Love is the mystery, the answer *and* the key to eternity.

44 God can be seen in the eyes of a beloved, in the delicate beauty of a flower, in the majesty of mountains, in the glory of a new day, in the vastness of the night sky... in you, in me, in everything.

45 Look, and *see* Yahweh.

46 Learn, and *know* Yahweh.

47 Touch, and *feel* Yahweh.

48 Love, and *be* Yahweh.

The Future Testament

Book Twelve: The Book of Eternity

Chapter 1
Called to Glory

1 Our thoughts of eternity will remain too small until the day our minds are perfectly merged with God, comprehending all.[1]

2 Our thoughts may yet be too small, but we are not small-minded.

3 We reach for the stars, seek the quark and expand π to trillions of digits.

4 We compose symphonies, create the internet, send satellites to the outer fringes of the solar system and feed the unfortunate.

5 We are one of Yahweh's crowning achievements, reflections of His transcendence.

6 On the journey of the soul we have come very far; we have oh so far to go.

7 We have learned much and yet have much to learn.

8 Picture yourself not so much on a journey as at a parade. Imagine yourself immoveable as the parade of life moves past you.

9 Absorbed in sacred devotion to holiness, in the forever here and now where God resides, we calmly watch the world spin.

10 God is here; God is now.

11 The passing parade of time, fashion and style is not real.

12 Only the Spirit, outside space and time, is eternally real.

13 And that Spirit, your sacred identity, is the source of your eternal life.

14 There has never been a time the *real* you did not exist, nor will there ever be a time when the *real* you ceases to exist.

---

[1] NT First Corinthians 13:12

15 Within the eternity of now, you are called to a destiny:

> *You have been called to the Glory of God!*[1]
> God's Glory is your true destiny,
> your real fruition and fulfillment.
> Lighting the spark of Holiness,
> Reborn to life in the Spirit,
> Christ's heart will beat as one with yours, and
> the mind of God will merge with yours,
> as Christ is formed in you, Divinity's Child.

16 Responding to this call embraces your totality. It is the pearl of great price Jesus spoke of, for which we should sell everything else.[2]

17 The life you lead is infinitely more important than a receptacle for "correct" beliefs.

18 Beliefs are a part of the parade of life's illusion.

19 Belief can lead to many great transformations, but only as a starting point.

20 There is nothing you can believe or disbelieve to find favor or disfavor with God.

21 Just as gravity is a Law that needs no agreement, and electromagnetism does not need your assent, so too is the Divine Law:

> Love is *union*.
> You *do* love God with your whole being,
> for your whole being *is* God.
> And you *do* love all people as yourself,
> for they *are* you.
> Your calling is to gain awareness of this,
> every moment of every day.

22 You are on a quest to learn what "you" means, to answer the call to ever-expanding empathy.

23 Loving yourself is only wrong when you love no one else.

24 Loving your family is only wrong when you love no other families.

25 It is only wrong to love your ethnicity when you love no other group.

---

[1] NT First Peter 5:10
[2] NT Matthew 13:45 & 46

26 It is only wrong to love your country when you love no other country.

27 The sin-trapped ego begins by identifying only with itself; the Spirit-led life identifies with *all*.[1]

28 What we do to the least of our sisters and brothers, we do to Christ *and to ourselves*. As Christ is formed in you, you become conscious that whatever is done to anyone is done to you.

29 The pathway to God-consciousness is best served with diligence, concentration and discipline. As Saint Paul said, "Work out your salvation with fear and trembling."[2]

Chapter 2
The Last Words on the Cross

1 Out of the unfathomable depths of time's formless void,[3] we awake on planet Earth bound to the wheel of time, as Christ Jesus was bound to the cross.

2 The scripture says, "We are united with Him in the likeness of his death, and resurrection."[4]

3 Ultimately, the *only* tools at our disposal to deal with the pains and disappointments of life are Jesus' last seven statements, the last words on the cross.

4 "I am thirsty."[5] The unquenched longing for water symbolizes our desire for peace, for God. If you have not yet known such thirst, *you will*.

5 Knowing the burn of thirst, our empathy grows, and we learn to have compassion for those around us who suffer the afflictions we have known.

6 "Woman, behold your son; son, behold your mother."[6] Jesus knew his time was at an end. In this statement he legally transferred responsibility for his mother to John, as his charge, to take care of her.

7 Even in death, compassion and concern for others, tangible and real, is the only way to God.

---

[1] NT Matthew 25:40, Galatians 3:28
[2] NT Philippians 2:12
[3] OT Genesis 1:2
[4] NT Romans 6:5
[5] NT John 19:38
[6] NT John 19:26

8 If you have never known or lived such loving compassion, *you will*.

9 "Father forgive them, for they do not know what they are doing."[1] Forgiveness is essential, etched into the very Heart of God.

10 Today, the Christ within us is calling us to a more radical forgiveness: we must be willing to forgive even though they *do know* what they are doing.

11 If you have never expressed such forgiveness, *you will*.

12 Be not deceived: the pathway is hard. "My God, my God, why have you forsaken me?"[2]

13 After healing, loving and teaching, sometimes our only immediate reward is suffering.

14 Never allow the trap of narcissism to ensnare you, mistakenly imagining that only pleasure will be your reward.

15 Follow the *true*, serve the *right*, and seek the *good*, not merely the *pleasant*.

16 Sometimes, in the dark night of your soul, it will seem as though God Himself has abandoned you.

17 If you have never known the dark night of the soul, *you will*.

18 But try always to retain hope.

19 "Truly, I say to you, today you will be with me in paradise."[3]

20 Try always to remember that everything, as designed, is very good.[4]

21 The reality of the Spirit is beauty.

22 Eventually, the delusions of life's parade will fall away, and we will return to paradise.

23 If you have never had a glimpse of the joys of perfect paradise, *you will*.

24 Then we will recognize our work in this world is done, and we say with Jesus, "It is finished."[5]

25 If you have never known this absolute peace of the Spirit, *you will*.

26 Our exhausted ego gasps its last, Christ is formed in us, and as a raindrop returning to the Infinite Ocean, we rejoice:

27 "Father, into Your hands I commit my spirit!" Your will, poured into the Greater Will of He Who Always Was, Is, and Will Be.

---

[1] NT Luke 23:34
[2] NT Matthew 27:46 and Mark 15:34
[3] NT Luke 23:43
[4] OT Genesis 1:31
[5] NT John 19:30

28 Not my way, but Yahweh.
29 I Will Be what I Will Be.
30 *You Will.*

Chapter 3
The Second Coming

1 When Jesus came to Earth, the Jewish people were looking for a military messiah who would conquer the Romans and establish Jerusalem as the kingly center of the world.

2 Jesus spent much of his ministry trying to explain that their vision of the messiah was incorrect.

3 Historically, we have sought solutions on the outside, with physical power, when God's real solutions are on the inside, spiritual.

4 After Jesus left, the people quickly returned to their old ways.

5 People *still* sought an earthly, physical messiah to establish an earthly, physical kingdom, using the earthly, physical power of violence.

6 And thus was born the notion of the second coming.

7 We now know that the language in the New Testament about the second coming must be highly symbolic because the moon cannot turn to blood.[1] It is impossible for the stars to fall to the Earth.[2]

8 Allow yourself the liberty to explore the symbolism in the New Testament. Determine for yourself what countless others have found:

As we were wrong about
the first coming of the messiah,
we have been wrong about
the second coming of the messiah.

9 The messiah never comes to establish physical kingdoms with military power. This is not the true pathway of God's loving forgiveness.

10 The first messiah's kingdom was not of this world, and neither is the coming of the second messiah.

---

[1] NT Acts 2:20
[2] NT Revelation 6:13

11 The second coming of Christ is when *you* are born again, living according to the Spirit, when Christ is formed in you.

12 Be in this world, but not of it.

13 The kingdom is not of this world.

14 The real kingdom is in you.

15 The true path has always been on the *inside*, sparked by rebirth and renewal of the mind.

16 Innocent as doves and shrewd as serpents,[1] we learn to wisely balance both the inner and outer worlds.

17 As Christ lives through you, *you* are the second coming of Christ.

Chapter 4
End Times

1 Jesus tried to be as clear as possible when he told us to spend *no time at all* worrying about tomorrow.[2]

2 Of course, for hundreds of years, the church has ignored him.

3 The world can be a very frightening place. Poverty, disease and war are just three of our constant unpleasant companions.

4 And we usually seek the easy way out.

5 The church decided it would be easier to passively wait for Jesus to "return" and fix all problems than to have to get involved with restoring Eden.

6 But it was never supposed to be that way.

7 From the first book of the Old Testament to the last book of the New Testament, we move from the Garden of Eden into the City of the New Jerusalem.

8 God builds the Garden; we help build the City.

9 We are co-creators with Yahweh, sparks of His infinity.

10 You must not be passive about your religion. You must not be passive about your life, the importance of the world or its inhabitants.

11 You must not be passive about the future.

12 Be clear: the best way to prepare for tomorrow is to fulfill all God calls you to, here and now, today.

13 Living today to the fullest is the best preparation for tomorrow.

---

[1] NT Matthew 10:16
[2] NT Matthew 6:34

14 Living fully involved in the *here and now* is the only preparation for eternal life.

15 God is here. God is now.

16 The end of the world cults that saw suffering as a cause for *rejoicing*, imagining calamity meant the imminent return of Jesus, fell into the most grievous error possible.

17 Never rejoice in another's suffering. Love them, and serve.

18 The end of the world is not cast in stone; it is waiting for us, Yahweh's co-creators.

19 All who have tried to predict the end of the world have been wrong. They always will be.

20 As the caterpillar makes his own cocoon, we move into the future we help create.

21 John's Revelation was a *warning*, not a promise.

22 Most, failing to properly understand the ancestral testaments, misunderstand one key point: the book of the Revelation contained symbolism that spoke clearly to people of Jesus' day.

23 It was precisely *because* of its pertinence that the Revelation was considered scripture.

24 Yet, for thousands of years, each era misunderstands Revelation as a roadmap to *their* immediate future.

25 They have always been wrong, and they have always been right.

26 The principal remains the same: the Revelation is *not* a roadmap to the external future, but it *is* a description of the internal kingdom.

27 As the second coming of Christ is an internal, spiritual event, so too Revelation is using symbolism in describing internal realities.

28 The spiritual message of the Revelation is always true:

> Things are bad,
> even worse than you think they are,
> and they are going to get worse still.
> But those who persevere to the end,
> who practice love and forgiveness,
> will regain access to The Tree of Life.

29 The Tree of Life has always been here, waiting for us to transcend ego, that we might feast deeply upon its fruit.

30 Forever it has been, and always will be: "Those who overcome will eat from the Tree of Life, which is in the Paradise of God."[1]

---

[1] NT Revelation 2:7

31 The leaves of the Tree of Life are for the healing of the nations.[1]
Yahweh longs for you to feed them to the world.

32 Amen.

Chapter 5
The Next World

1 Our notions about the next world, what Shakespeare's Hamlet calls "the undiscovered country," are intentionally kept small by a merciful God.

2 The realms of life after death are *meant* to be a mystery.

3 To prepare for tomorrow, fully live today. Likewise, to prepare for the next life, fully live this one.

4 You have what Yahweh wants you to have. If He wanted you to have clear memories of the next world, you would have them.

5 After their marvelous nuptials, the bride and groom must, in some measure, forget the bliss of their honeymoon in order to return to their regular jobs.

6 We have work to do here on Earth; we have lessons to learn.

7 We, too, must forget the bliss of heaven in order to concentrate on our duties in this world.

8 Yet we cannot help but wonder: what will we find on the other side of mortality's veil?

9 Thousands of people die every year, and are medically recalled to life. They relate very similar stories of being greeted by loved ones, tunnels of light and extreme feelings of bliss.

10 Almost all near-death survivors relate that the next world feels *more* real than this one.

11 Technology has given us a clue about the reality of the timeless next world:

12 A movie has its own era (when the movie takes place) and its own flow of time, but none of it is *real*. In the experience of the movie, time *appears* real. But our world is even *more* real than the movie, and our time stands "outside" the time frame of the movie.

13 Learn the parable of the movie: the next world relates to this one, as our world relates to a movie.

---

[1] NT Revelation 22:2

14 The greatest mystery about life after death is how much the next world is like this one.

15 Death does *not* magically "complete" or perfect you. This is a great misunderstanding championed by the ways of old.

16 Learn the parable of the automobile: you relate to your car exactly the same way your soul relates to your body.

17 When you are done with your journey, you step out of the car and remain the same person.

18 When you are done with life's journey, you exit your physical body and remain the same person.

19 When you die, you remain exactly as you were in life, minus a physical body.

20 After death you have the same thoughts, feelings, hopes and desires you have in this life. Your consciousness remains the same.

21 The real purpose of your physical body is to provide *training wheels* for your soul, a buffer between your desires and your actions.

22 In this world, action requires *will* plus *thought* plus *desire* plus the *physical* action. You can want something very much and yet not do it.

23 In the next world, the final step, the buffer between desire and action, is lost. *Will* plus *thought* plus *desire* equals our actions in the next world.

24 This is why the scripture says, "Delight yourself in the will of Yahweh, and He will give you the desires of your heart."[1] In the next world, desire is action.

25 This is why Jesus tried to get us to pay attention to our inner world; when we have desire, *it is the same as if we have done it!*[2]

26 The life you live matters, in this world, and the next.

27 Much more could be said, but little else matters. Seek first for God, His kingdom and righteousness;[3] everything else, in this world and the next, will be added to you at the perfect time.

---

[1] OT Psalm 37:4
[2] NT Matthew 5:28
[3] NT Matthew 6:33

Chapter 6
Worship

1 Worship is performed most perfectly in utter privacy, in fellowship with all Divinity's Children.

2 Loving God and loving each other is beautifully expressed in worship: each soul in communion with the Divine, united in the company of beloved brothers and sisters.

3 Individual and group, public and private, forever one.

4 Only the trivial-minded ask if you need to go to church to go to heaven. The question itself is wrong. The correct question is,

5 "Do I need to be involved in a faith community in order to grow in the Spirit?" And the answer is, "Yes, of course."

6 In our infancy, we go where our parents take us.

7 In our youth, we attend whatever church will feed us spiritually.

8 In our maturity, we seek people *we can help.*

9 Having been blessed, we seek to bless others.

10 The cycles work as systems[1] and forever remain true: we start in ignorance, then learn and eventually teach.

11 We begin poor, gain wealth and find fulfillment in sharing with others.

12 Born in darkness, we seek the light and then shine as a light to the world.

13 We start sick, gain health and participate in healing the nations with the leaves on the Tree of Life.

14 Paul admonishes us to pray always.[2] Obviously, he does not mean we should spend our life on our knees by the side of a bed.

15 Rather, our entire life can be a living prayer.

16 Seek to make every idea, every hope and every desire a prayer for love, joy, peace and goodness. This is your *private* expression of worship.

17 Whether you eat or drink, whatever you do in word or deed, do it to the glory of God.[3] This is your *public* expression of worship.

18 There is no sacrifice you can give, no mystical meditation you can perform, that could ever be as important as taking care of your family and acting honorably in business.

19 The life you lead matters.

---

[1] FT Liberty Chapter 1
[2] NT First Thessalonians 5:17
[3] NT First Corinthians 10:31, Colossians 3:17

20 Service to family and strangers is the highest form of worship.

21 When you gather together in public, beware the pitfalls of performance. Beautiful buildings, with inspired singers, talented instrumentalists and compensated speakers, do *not* necessarily constitute worship; it is a performance, a show, a paid concert.

22 Worship allows the common people to speak, to sing, to share. Each is perfect in their simple honesty.

23 There is great strength in the common people, for Yahweh lives in each of us.

24 Jesus met with the simplest folk. We will find great strength in following his wise example.

25 The Future Testament invites you to transcend performance and return to sharing fellowship.

26 As there is strength in the common people, there is great value in common life.

Chapter 7
The Breath of God

1 Our notions about God will *not* always be too small.

2 Countable and uncountable infinity, eternity beyond time, transrational numbers, a physical Universe of billions of galaxies, sub-atomic particles, a Tree of Life that records every event, thought and desire from every living being…

3 It will take forever to absorb the True, Right and Good of God.

4 But you have enough time. You have eternal life.

5 When you are really ready, you will find the next door to consciousness has already been opened for you.

6 And when you *step through* that door, you will find love, forever growing, forever deepening.

7 Love will be perfected. Joy will be made whole.

8 Peace will come; peace will reign.

9 In realms beyond time, we will know everything. *Everything.*

10 We will know as much about God as God knows about us.[1]

11 But who can have such knowledge? It is too high for ego.

12 Only the Mind of God can know the thoughts of God.[2]

13 In that perfect day, the cycle will be complete, and God will fully know God as God.

---

[1] NT First Corinthians 13:12
[2] NT First Corinthians 2:11

14 As you give, you receive.

15 So if you really want God, you must *give* God.

16 To get God, you must live God.

17 This is the Breath of God.[1]

18 God has died so you can live. When you are ready to respond, and die to ego, God will live in and through you.

19 Divinity's Children will find themselves where they have always been: in the Heart of Infinite Yahweh, feasting on the Tree of Life, drinking deeply from the River of Life.

20 But of all the mysteries, this much can be known now, with utter certainty:

21 In the end, there will be fulfillment.[2]

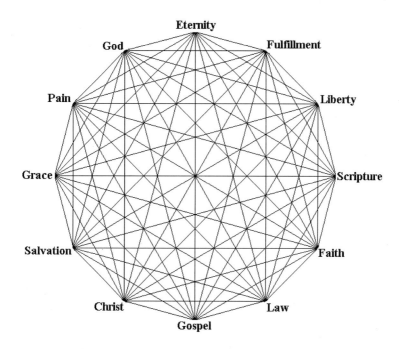

---

[1] FT God 3:24
[2] FT Fulfillment 1:1

Blank page for notes

The Future Testament

Supplements

Introduction to the Supplements

The people who assembled the Future Testament thought it best to provide the supplemental background materials that follow.

As with the Future Testament itself, this material is completely optional.

The Future Testament is based on a relatively small collection of core ideas, presented in the following pages for the people who may not be familiar with this approach to life, God, the Bible and religion. For some, these supplements may be intuitively obvious and reading them will be unnecessary, while for others it may be new material and vital to their understanding of the text.

Jesus asserts that the only way to the Father is through *truth*. Some of the material here addresses the grievous errors that have befallen Christianity. We now stand two thousand years removed from the life of Jesus, and over the years misperceptions and mistakes have most assuredly crept into our traditions. So, if some of the ideas presented in the Future Testament or these supplements seem to threaten or attack notions you have held sacred, we encourage you to look into these matters for yourself.

But please know that we mean no harm or disrespect. Only love. Love for you, love for God, love for Christ and love for truth.

Finally, the materials presented here are not meant to be exhaustive treatments of the subjects. All of the topics are overviews and outlines, meant to point you in the direction of deeper personal study and growth.

As always, we encourage you to research, seek and discover as much as possible about God, our glorious Universe and the beauties of humanity. To this end, we pray that this material may be of help to you.

We offer it with humble love.

--The Future Testament Staff

Supplement 1:
Religion and the Scientific Method

"I am my beloved's and he is mine."[1]

Crystals grow from a single molecule that attaches to innumerable other molecules until a wonderfully beautiful structure has developed. A snowflake crystal grows from countless water molecules, which freeze and attach themselves together in a pattern unique among all other snowflakes. Thus, at the heart of every crystal there is one essential molecule from which everything else derives.

This supplement, *Religion and the Scientific Method*, is the central molecule from which the Future Testament and all its supplemental documents arise.

All people in the industrialized worlds of the 21st century C.E. are children of divorce. As children of divorce, we bear upon our psyches the scars of that tragedy. The divorce we speak of is the divorce of the heart from the mind, the divorce of reason from emotion, the divorce of belief from action, the divorce of religion from science.

The purpose of the Future Testament is to heal this rift, to further the reunion of the heart and mind on the individual level, and religion and science on the global level.

In the days of the ancestral Testaments Old and New, there were no distinctions between philosopher, theologian, scientist and spiritual seeker. There were simply those who worked and those who thought, those who trudged through life and those who explored life. The explorers found religious significance in every scientific discovery, and every scientific discovery was a gateway to new understandings about the cosmos, and therefore God. Realizations that impressed themselves on the minds of the explorers would of necessity lead to action, and every action was inspired by an emotional, religious, spiritual calling.

The great event of Christianity (either its greatest blessing or greatest curse) was when Constantine, Emperor of Rome, made Christianity the state religion in the early 300s. The church became both the religious

---

[1] OT The Song of Solomon 6:3

and the civil authority, leading to a situation where all power and money flowed through this one organization. Over the course of time, the church lost its totalitarian power as society went through a scientific revolution typified most clearly by Galileo and Copernicus, who made it known that the Earth was not the center of the Universe. The church refused to vary from dogmatic pronunciations of the past and found itself trapped. For the church to embrace this new information meant there was a possibility that the church had been wrong about things in the past, and therefore something was potentially wrong with things the church was saying now. Rather than face the challenge of the new realization of truth contained in the modern heliocentric view of the world, the church rejected it outright, branded Galileo a heretic and excommunicated him. Although an oversimplification, the great divorce was born in that decision.

Humankind's quest for truth then fractured into at least two primary camps: those who sought the truths of God, the heart and the spirit (religion), and those who sought the truths of the natural world, astronomy and physics (science). At the dawn of the 21st century, we are beginning to see signs that the two great traditions are starting to reconcile, yet there is much more work that needs to be done.

We have come to realize it best to speak of knowledge in terms of three great domains:

that which is *true*, that which is *right* and that which is *good*.

The *true* is the "it" world: the objectivity of electromagnetism, mathematics, chemistry, etc.

The *right* is the intersubjectivity of "we." Certainly, it is *right* to not murder, yet this is a social convention which cannot and does not stand with the same objective autonomy found in the realm of the *true*. The "we" of the *right* helps to define the different ways that human beings interact with one another, declaring what is socially acceptable.

The *good* is the subjectivity of "I". This is private personal preference. I think Beethoven is *good*, but you prefer Mozart.

True	It	External	Science	Objective
Right	We	Shared	Morality	Intersubjective
Good	I	Internal	Art	Subjective

In the course of human interactions, the true, the right and the good become confused. We take a personal *good*, our personal preference from the realm of "I," and declare our good to be good for everyone. The good therefore becomes the right. "Because I think spaghetti is good, everyone should eat spaghetti and not salad." This is the beginning of tyranny. From there it becomes easy for those in power to declare that the *good* and the *right* have become the *true:* "Since I prefer spaghetti, everyone should only eat spaghetti, and it is therefore the will of God that spaghetti is the only true food."

Realizing the confusion among the relationships of the *true*, the *right* and the *good* is indispensable as we move forward in examining our traditional religious structures and current social and ecclesiastical systems.

The Scientific Method

During the great divorce, the mind of humanity created a system for the pursuit of knowledge which is a greater accomplishment than any specific knowledge gained from following the system. The system known as the *scientific method* establishes a series of steps by which we can come to shared experience, with the certainty of verifiable knowledge. Pontius Pilate famously asked Jesus, "What is truth?" The scientific method explains the steps by which one can come to the understanding of truth. Although there is no universal approach to the scientific method, it generally constitutes eight distinct yet interrelated steps.

1. **Observation**. We see birds and stars. We observe elephants acting strangely after eating a particular fruit. We see people die. We observe as the Sun becomes eclipsed.

2. **Questioning**. We begin to question not only what that big orange thing in the sky *is*, but what it is made of. How long has it been there? How far away is it? How does it move? It seems to change positions from summer to winter. Beyond the what, we ask why? Why can birds fly? Why is the Sun hot? Why do we die?

3. **Hypothesis**. We come up with an educated guess in answer to our question. "It seems that the most likely answer is..." Hypothesis can be nothing more than a hunch, based upon our observations or upon reason. A hypothesis is an informed guess.

4. **Research.** Are there others who have had this observation, asked these questions and come up with pertinent hypotheses before? Research is a crucial area where community is of vital importance. The research component of the scientific method means we are aware of what has come before us. We must have access to the results of those who precede us, or we cannot make any real progress. At best, we might repeat their results, but that will not advance human knowledge.

5. **Experiment.** The experiment is the core of the scientific method. This is where we test our hypothesis. We actually combine two chemicals to see what happens. We roll a ball down a slope to determine how long it takes to get to the bottom. We plot the motion of a planet as it moves across the sky. The experiment happens with the use of our minds and senses. As we move further into the realms of the unknown, the experiment happens with the use of intermediary instruments. For example, microscopes and telescopes have allowed us to venture further into the realms of experimentation and observation than we were able to with our bio-senses. Our ever-expanding technology provides us the opportunity to perceive truths beyond the limits of our biophysical bodies.

6. **Analysis.** After our experimentation, we have a whole new set of observations. We then begin to recycle the process because the scientific method is a constant iterative process of observation, experiment and analysis. Why did the ball roll down the track for exactly 7.2 seconds? Why is it that the Sun stops moving south along the horizon precisely on December 21st? We take our experiment and determine the extent to which our results confirm or dispute our initial hypothesis.

7. **Evaluation and verification.** When we come to a result that seems valid, knowing our experiment is sound and our techniques and tools are pure, we are able to evaluate the data—not just the "what" but the "whys." Do we have a sound experiment that tells us something, whether true or false, about our hypothesis? We may repeat the experiment numerous times in order to evaluate and verify our results to our satisfaction.

8. **Publish the results.** This is a crucial step that again involves community. We publish our results so that those who come after

us can learn from us, just as we have learned from those who came before us.

Although this is an oversimplified sketch of the scientific method, it shows the process by which we develop knowledge. The scientific method is an *epistemological* (meaning the study of the nature of knowledge) approach. The goal of research is to come to *verifiable knowledge* because knowledge must be experienced by others, or else it cannot be considered knowledge.

Recipe, Experience, Community

The validation of knowledge consists of three aspects, which are the goal and essence of the scientific method.

1. First is the *recipe*, or a series of steps to follow. For example, the recipe might be to take a piece of glass, form it a certain way and point it toward a particular object in the sky: you will see the rings of Saturn. The recipe says, "Do this exact thing and you will get this result." The key to the recipe's instructions is *to gain an experience*. "Do ABC, and XYZ will happen." The recipe is the heart and soul of both the experiment and the observations. If you perform *this* experiment with *these* tools in *this* way, then you will get *this* result. If you get a different result, we do not have verified knowledge. Perhaps one of our experiments was flawed. Perhaps the recipe was not followed correctly. Perhaps an instrument was misaligned. There may be many different reasons we could get different results when it comes to verifying the knowledge from the experiment.

2. The second component in the validation of knowledge is *direct experience*. For the recipe to be valid, it must lead directly to a specific incident. I have to be able to directly encounter the process *and* the results of the experiment in order to determine that it is indeed verified. Sometimes this immediacy will involve the senses, while other times it will be a systematic, logical knowing, as in a mathematical proof. Simply having or taking someone else's word is not sufficient. Believing someone's statement that steps ABC result in XYZ is *not* verification. This is not validation. There must be an actual, repeatable experience of XYZ resulting from ABC. If you want to know that Saturn is not just a dot in the sky but is actually an amazing structure with a set of rings around

it, you must follow certain steps (the recipe) leading to a direct experience, and you will see the rings of Saturn for yourself. The *recipe* leads to *direct experience.*

3. The third component of validated knowledge is *community*, the whole realm of sharing, publishing and confirming with one another that what we have experienced is real. I may have made a serious mistake or operated under an unknown assumption, in order to have my ABC generate XYZ. Without the community step, even if the knowledge gained is valid and true, it remains a private matter and is of no use to the human race. We owe the human race the benefit of our results because without the platform of our experience, those who come after us make no progress.

Recipe, experience, community. This is the heart of the scientific method and the method by which humans have progressed for millennia.

Religion as Science

The preceding material may seem utterly foreign to a book as devoutly religious as the Future Testament, and that is entirely the point.

As we said, religion and science were *united* at the beginning. The prophets were the priests and also the experimenters. During history's earliest examinations of mathematics and geometry, participants in the knowledge were initiated into a sacred society full of all the normal religious trappings: rituals, secret signs and symbols, etc.

If we look to the Old and New Testaments, the threefold aspects of verifiable knowledge (recipe, experiment and community) can be clearly seen:

1. *Recipe.* "Keep his decrees and commands, which I am giving you today, so that it may go well with you and your children after you and that you may live long in the land Yahweh your God gives you for all time."[1] "So *if* you faithfully obey the commands I am giving you today [to love Yahweh your God and to serve him with all your heart and with all your soul] *then* I will send rain on your land in its season... and you will eat and be satisfied."[2]

---

[1] OT Deuteronomy 4:40
[2] OT Deuteronomy 11:11 - 13

2. *Experience.* "Taste and see that Yahweh is good."[1] "Blessed are the pure in heart, for they will see God."[2] "Touch me and see, a ghost does not have flesh and bones, as you see I have."[3]

3. *Community.* "All the believers were one in heart and mind..."[4] "When the day of Pentecost came, they were all together in one place."[5]

The entire book of Deuteronomy is structured around verifiable knowledge. The *recipe* of Deuteronomy is "do this and live." The *experiment* is the life of faith of the people of Israel. The history of Israel can be seen as a prolonged *experiment*, testing the *recipe* and sharing the results in the *community*. Some live what is written, and some do not.

Jesus was not just giving sweet little sayings to make us feel good, but rather admonishing us to follow his recipe and verify his knowledge. "If you wish to come after me, then take up your cross and follow me" is Jesus' recipe for the experience. We are called to follow Jesus' recipe with our own lives in order to experience the truth of this new life in the Spirit. Then we share our experiences with our the church, our ecclesiastical community.

The early church was full of people who followed Jesus' recipe. Their faith in Jesus provided a hope for their own lives: essentially a hypothesis based upon faith, which led to a series of steps that they could validate with their lives, to experience the truth of Jesus' recipe. Their results were published in the Bible: verifiable knowledge of *recipe, experience and community.*

---

[1] OT Psalm 34:8
[2] NT Matthew 5:8
[3] NT Luke 24:39
[4] NT Acts 4:32
[5] NT Acts 2:1

I Am the Truth

Let's look at Jesus' saying from the Gospel of John. "I am the way, the truth and the life. No one comes to the Father but by me."[1] For clarity, we will remove the compound nature of his statement and turn it into three:

> "I am the *way*. No one comes to the Father but by me."
> "I am the *truth*. No one comes to the Father but by me."
> "I am the *life*. No one comes to the Father but by me."

Essentially, these three statements are an expression of the scientific method and the three aspects of verifiable knowledge: recipe, experience and community:

> "I am the *recipe*. No one comes to the Father but by me."
> "I am the *experience*. No one comes to the Father but by me."
> "I am the *community*. No one comes to the Father but by me."
>
> "I am the recipe, the experience and the community. No one comes to the Father but by me."

Recipe. "I am the way. No one comes to the Father but by me." This is not simply an idea, a poem or a beautiful picture: Jesus is talking about a *way*, a *process,* a *path* or a *journey*. What Jesus and genuine religion speak of is a recipe, a way to be *followed*. Jesus is talking about the *way* to move from our first birth (the name, religion, language and heritage of our parents) into the second birth, which is not of nature but of the Spirit. The new life is no longer lived according to what society dictates, but by God's leading. You are to become a star child, a child of the Universe—all that God wants you to be. This is the "way" Jesus is describing.

"I am the way. No one comes to the Father but by me" is a recipe. If you do A, B and C (follow this way), then you will know X,Y and Z (come to the Father).

Experience. "I am the truth. No one comes to the Father but by me." Jesus is talking about an experience, a verifiable knowing. Jesus' way is not to simply sit around and let him handle life for you. His is a living *way* that leads to an experience of truth. You *can* have verifiable knowledge. You can have the experience of seeing your life change,

---

[1] NT John 14:6

the experience of resurrection and the experience of the pearl of great price. Jesus is not asking you to accept anything simply on faith, but to follow the journey yourself, taking his way. If you follow the *way* of ABC, it will lead you to the living experiential *truth* of XYZ.

Truth *is* what sets us free. Truth *is* the way to the Father. "I am the truth. No one comes to the Father but by the truth." Many seem happy to live a comfortable lie rather than face a painful truth. Still, only truth can lead us to God. Only truth can lead us to the renaissance of the human spirit.

Truth that leads to the renaissance of the human spirit is why the Supplements include material about the ancestral testaments, in order to move us beyond biblical "inerrancy." Though these may be uncomfortable notions for some, the Future Testament maintains that *truth is the only religion*. Only truth will take us to God.

Community. "I am the life. No one comes to the Father but by me." The life you live is the way to God. It is only through living that we become God-conscious.

It is not enough to have thoughts or feelings or even knowledge; verifiable knowledge is *life*, a life we share with all around us.

All of your *life* is involved in your *way* to finding the *truth* of God. Only balanced, real life can come to the Father. Please see the supplement **The Four Aims of Life** for more about living a balanced life.

Jesus' recipe leads us to a truth, a living experiment that will set us free from the restrictions of society. We can lead lives fully imbued with physical, emotional and mental health, properly balanced with the four aims of life.

> **Beliefs, doctrines, dogmas, confessions and creeds**
> **that have nothing to do with life**
> **should have nothing to do with religion.**
> **If they do not touch your life, do not touch them.**

Dogma Abandons Verifiable Knowledge

We now come to the main problem.

When the great divorce between science and religion happened, the church could not admit there might be something wrong with its views and teachings. Therefore, unable to change with the times, religion could not participate in or celebrate with the community outside the castle walls of the church. The community outside was going through an unbelievable change of perspective about who we are and what the Universe is all about. As a result, the church divorced itself from life.

Growing humanity's new verifiable knowledge of sky, sea and self was denounced by the church. Since the church could not even admit what was verifiable, it could no longer celebrate "the way, the truth and the life" and *relegated itself to the untouchable and indefensible*: doctrines and dogmas.

The cult of belief was born.

Christianity had always had proclamations, beliefs and creeds. But these were connected, through the ministry of the church, to all aspects of life: hospitals, universities and almost all branches of knowledge were extensions of the life of faith. Feeding the poor, healing the sick and the life you lived still mattered.

But the cult of belief was something different. Divorced from the scientific revolution and verifiable knowledge, the church relegated itself to what could not be questioned or tested.

Dogmatic life, simply giving agreement to doctrines and dogmas, fails to touch the three essential aspects of verifiable knowledge.

In some dogmas, for example, you must believe that Jesus was born of a biological virgin. Many people have died for being unable to say they agree with this belief. Notice how this belief fails to touch the three strands of verifiable knowledge:

1. *No recipe.* Whether I do or do not believe in the biological virgin birth is not going to touch any part of my life! There is nothing for me to *do* so that I can experience and then know—there is simply an abstract externalized doctrine to which I am expected to give assent.

2. *No experience.* Whether I do or do not believe that Jesus was born of a biological virgin will give me no experience, pro or con.

3. *No communal life to share.* It does not touch me or any aspect of my life—not my heart or my mind, not my money or relaxation or social service or even my quest for God. It is simply what is written down in an ancient book that I'm expected to accept.

Believing Jesus was born of a biological virgin does not create community, other than a shallow connection with others who also believe that Jesus was born of a biological virgin.

The cult of belief's doctrines and dogmas, declaring and demanding that the only pathway to heaven is to believe certain doctrines, *fail the primary strands of verifiable knowledge.* Doctrines and dogmas wind up being useless to living our lives. Life is what matters.

Your life matters.

"I am the way. No one comes to the Father but by me. I am truth. No one comes to the Father but by me. I am life. No one comes to the Father but by me."[1]

No one comes to the Father except through truth. No one comes to the Father except by following the way, the way which is life. Your assent to an ancient dogma will *not* get you to the Father.

Life Matters

If it does not touch your life, do not touch it.

Religion and spirituality in the 21st century are failing to touch life. There are no significant metrics by which people *inside* the church are in any way sociologically distinguishable from those *outside* it. Divorce, child abuse, drug use, suicide, alcoholism and debt are all essentially identical *inside* and *outside* the Christian community.

Clearly, something has gone wrong.

Ancient dogmas no longer touch life, if ever they did.

Useless doctrine and dogma are not limited to ancient documents, however. There are plenty of modern-day texts that purport to be life-changing but will not *really* touch your life, including popular books providing all sorts of interesting ideas about the formation of the Earth, the vibratory frequencies of realms beyond, etc. We have access to an excess of material that cannot be verified, does not offer any recipes for gaining personal experience and therefore fails the central test of being a valid pursuit of knowledge. This does not mean that such books are wrong or evil, but they cannot and will not generate genuine reform in life because they are little more than chatter with no connection to

---

[1] NT John 14:6, slightly rearranged.

anything in life that truly matters. Failing to be a *way*, they contain no verifiable *truth*, cannot touch your *life*, and cannot lead to the Father.

> **If it does nothing else, the Future Testament wants to help you re-examine your own life by offering a living way for you to experience verifiable truth and knowledge. This is why the Future Testament is not interested in giving you a new batch of beliefs to argue about, but rather an entirely new way of approaching religion. And it's not really a new way at all, but rather a way identical to that of the patriarchs, prophets and saints of old, the same verifiable knowledge pathway that Jesus demonstrated and championed.**

Another approach to think about this *way* is through the notion of Occam's Razor. Occam was a famous scientist in the great divorce who essentially said that the simplest answer is usually going to be the best answer. In other words, we don't need all sorts of intangible beliefs about magical tablets, mystical visions or mythic kingdoms. *Entrance into heaven cannot depend upon belief in someone else's ancient vision.* True religion is to take care of the poor, feed the hungry and visit the lonely.

If it doesn't touch your life, do not touch it.

Isaiah asked, "Why are you willing to work for what is not food, and labor for what does not satisfy?"[1] Why do we put our endless religious energies into what amounts to 21st-century versions of "How many angels can dance on the head of a pin?"

True Religion

True religion must return to verifiable knowledge. If the human race is going to make progress, we must return to the ways of old—not to believe what they believed, but rather to live our lives in accordance with searching for verifiable knowledge of God.

This might seem hard (if not impossible) for many reasons. At this point in history, the expectation that religion is only about belief, doctrines and events that *cannot* be proven has been around so long it has almost become part of our DNA.

---

[1] OT Isaiah 55:2

The Future Testament is here to say that applying the scientific method to religion is not only *possible*; it is vitally *necessary*. Finding ways to apply the three aspects of verifiable knowledge (recipe, experience and community) to religion is not only *possible*; it is *essential*.

Early humanity found everything to be sacred. To early humanity, everything had a tangible connection to the life they lived and was an extension of the Divine. Life itself was the way to draw close and experience God. Through the great divorce, we separated our heads from our hearts. Now, through the process of applying the scientific method to verifiable knowledge, we will find the great reunification of our people and our society. The supplemental document **Resacralization** discusses this concept.

Mathematics as Bridge

For some, the proposition of using the scientific method for religion is absurd. Science (it is said) applies to what is tangible: what I can actually experience with my senses, assisted by technology. Religion (it is said) is the realm of the intangible: hopes, fears and irrational *beliefs*.

But this is simply not true, or at least it should not be.

No one would deny that mathematics is one of the sciences, yet mathematics is essentially a "religion" of science. Mathematics deals with intangibles. Mathematics deals with very little that can be physically manipulated; any physical manipulation is just an *example*, not the real thing. You can look at a triangle all day long, but the triangle itself will not prove to you the Pythagorean theorem, $A^2 + B^2 = C^2$. The real truths of mathematics are abstract, nonphysical and symbolic, but they are nevertheless able to be subjected to verifiable knowledge and the three strands of recipe, result and community! The notion of a parabola and its mathematical properties can be studied in the abstract and then applied to building real, tangible satellite dishes.

The truth of the science of mathematics lies beyond what is tangible.

Notice the striking parallels:

The highest truths of religion (life after death, faith, God) do not deal with anything that you can physically manipulate. You can look at the Universe all day long, but it will not prove to you that God exists. The real truths of religion are abstract, nonphysical and symbolic, but they are nevertheless able to be subjected to verifiable knowledge and the three strands of recipe, result and community! The notion of resurrection and the properties of faith can be studied in the abstract and then applied to your real, actual life.

The truths of both the science of mathematics *and* religion lie beyond what is tangible.

So, applying the scientific method to religion is to search for what lies outside what we can see, touch, smell or taste. And yet, as we perceive these abstract truths, like freedom, inspiration of scripture, fulfillment and life after a death, these *abstract* truths *can and will touch us deeply in our regular lives.*

Thoughts, ideas and beliefs that cannot be transformed into some form of verifiable knowledge that affects your life are outside the scope of this document. With all humility, we propose that such notions should also be outside the scope of your life.

Assumptions Shape Everything

We are capable of knowing things and being able to prove them on the basis of reason, rationality and logic.

But underlying all of our reason, rationality and logic, we come to our assumptions: things we hold to be true but cannot prove (Note: advanced seekers may be greatly interested in examining the notion of axioms in the light of Gödel's Incompleteness Theorem, wherein he proved that there are valid truths we can *know* but cannot *prove*).

In mathematics, we start with axioms, also called postulates or assumptions. Axioms can be neither proven nor disproven. For example, the parallel line postulate says that two parallel lines remain equidistant forever, and you can either accept this or not. Perhaps they meet at infinity, or I could assume they become infinitely apart. It is a choice. What I assume about parallel lines becomes a part of the *definition.* Everything we do with parallel lines ultimately rests on a decision, a choice, a definition which is an unprovable assumption. "When I use a word," Humpty Dumpty said in rather a scornful tone, "it means just what I choose it to mean—neither more nor less."[1]

---

[1] Lewis Carroll's *Through the Looking Glass*, Chapter 6.

Invariably, religious disagreements and political arguments (and nearly all controversial topics) rely on their underlying *assumptions.* Unaware of our reliance on these assumptions, or even their *existence*, we are at a loss to explain how the other person can be so *stupid.* But if the dialogue can ever proceed from a rational discussion of our unnamed assumptions, we will find that we simply start from fundamentally different perspectives, themselves irreconcilable.

This is the essence of the current antipathy between religion and science: they start from irreconcilable and opposite assumptions, both currently unprovable:

> Science says that the ultimate reality is energy/mass and that consciousness is a function of chemical reactions in the brain.

> Religion says that the ultimate reality is
> the consciousness of a trans-material Being
> and that energy/mass (the material Universe)
> is a function of that consciousness.

The ramifications of these differences are countless. But this assumption is the heart of it all:

> Science assumes (and cannot prove) that
> energy/mass is the ultimate reality,
> while religion assumes (and cannot prove) that
> God is the ultimate reality.

At the very least, we owe it to ourselves and each other to be aware of our assumptions and to state them.

The Two Axioms

All of the material in the Future Testament is based upon two axioms:

Axiom 1: God exists.

At this point, it is not possible to *prove* God exists. The basis of this work is that there is a super-conscious essence that has given shape to everything that exists. Consciousness is first; the brain comes later.

Axiom 2: The super-conscious entity (God) exists in a relational connection to humanity.

In other words, the Hermetic aphorism 'As above, so below' is true. This world *says something* about its source, like a painting says something about the artist or a book says something about its author. And what we learn "down here" can lead to valid observations about the God who is "up there."

One property of fractals is that each tiny part fully embodies the attributes of the whole. Axiom 2 states, in essence, that everything here *below* exists in a fractal relationship to everything *above*. Parables are a valid way of learning about God because of Axiom 2. The Universe can be seen as a parable. Everything we learn about the Universe can teach us something about God.

Everything in the Future Testament flows from these Axioms.

Parables

As an example, let's look at the notion of God as perfect parent. Axiom 1 tells us that God exists. From hamsters to birds to humans, we know how essential parents are. So, Axiom 2 suggests that parenting tells us something significant about God. We still have to deal with what a perfect parent would be and map that to how (theoretically) God "behaves" towards us. That can be found in the text of the Future Testament.

If we are comfortable that a decent model for understanding our relationship to the Divine is exactly what the ancients, Jesus and most of the world's religions have said, that God is our Heavenly Parent, then certain conclusions can be reached that will both support and repudiate different aspects of our current religious thinking.

If God exists and "as above, so below" is real, then what we see here *below* tells us something about what is *above.* Thus, the laws of conservation tell us something about God. The cycle of evaporation can tell us something about God. The way a tree grows tells us something about God. The psalmist is exactly right: "The heavens declare the glory of God and the Earth shows his handiwork."[1]

In this way, then, the Future Testament seeks to apply the scientific method to religion. The two Axioms lead to observations, and our research connects us to the ancients who have come before us, what the Book of Hebrews calls the "great cloud of witnesses."[2] We then apply our life as a living hypothesis, examine our conclusions and share our

---

[1] OT Psalm 19:1
[2] NT Hebrews 12:1

results with those around us. Recipe, experience, and community: the scientific method applied to religion, to gain verifiable knowledge of *life.*

The Future Testament has no fear of science. Truth is one. Whatever the *reality* of energy/mass/consciousness/God, only that reality matters. Truth is the only religion. All of materialistic science can lead us to an incredible treasure chest of parables.

Language plays a great role in our knowledge about God. The greater our vocabulary, the more we can understand and express. As we learn more and more about the physical Universe, we are able to learn more and more about the spiritual Universe. More about this idea can be found in the supplement **Truth in Embryo**.

Word and name are directly related to the role of language. We have a trinity: that which is named; the name; and the thoughts, feelings and impressions the name brings to the listener. The three are one: what is named, the name and the person who is receiving and interpreting the name.

God's Name is one of the deepest and most profound ideas we can contemplate, and it has very much to do with our lives. For greater understanding of this concept, please see the supplement **God's Name Yahweh.**

Meditation on God's Name will bring us closer to God. Meditation on the Universe can, will and should bring us closer to God. This is the birth of all parables and the resacralization of the world. This is the pathway to the remarriage of science and religion and the reunification of mind and heart.

It is the purpose of the Future Testament.

For Further Reading

We highly recommend "*The Marriage of Sense and Soul: Integrating Science and Religion*" by Ken Wilber, © 1998 Random House and Broadway Books, New York.

Supplement 2:
The Four Aims of Life

Religion should not be abstract, nor should it be merely intellectual. The true spiritual life must touch and affect every part of our existence. The difficulty of the modern condition is that our society makes it almost impossible to live in anything other than a fractured way. We send our soldiers to hurt, maim and kill, then expect them to come home and peacefully hug the kids and pet the dog. The corporate life only seems less violent because the attacks and defenses of corporations are removed from personal responsibility.

It should not be this way. The great Hebrew proclamation, "Hear O Israel, Yahweh is our God, Yahweh is One,"[1] is telling us we *should* and *must* lead a unified life. Hypocrisy, saying one thing and doing another, cannot live in the heart of a truly devoted lover of God.

But this oneness goes much farther than resisting hypocrisy. Our jobs, recreation, friends, family and faith life must all work together, as *one*. How we earn our money should seamlessly integrate with how we spend it.

Those who claim they are "spiritual but not religious" miss the point of both. You cannot have a spiritual life isolated from the rest of your experience, nor can you be a spiritual person without fellowship, for the true spirit is that which unites us: love. The essence of the Great Law is to love God and to love one another, and this love cannot be extended in isolation on the proverbial desert island. So people who claim they are "spiritual but not religious" have very often substituted the true life of spirit for narcissism: whatever feels good is what they call "spirituality." However, to live a genuine spirit-filled life, you must find your way into some form of religious community, a gathering of souls that practices together in fellowship and friendship. It is essential to be involved with the lives of our fellow human beings, as such fellowship is absolutely mandatory to being a spiritual person.

Understandably, very often people think of the term 'religion' in a negative way, as though it implies singing in incomprehensible dead

---

[1] OT Deuteronomy 6:4

languages while incense burners swing out clouds of fragrant smoke, in stained-glass-windowed halls with golden tapestries and old men in funny-looking robes. This need not be religion.

> In its roots, religion simply means to get re-connected.

Religion is anything that reconnects us to God and our fellow human beings; in other words, it is anything that fulfills the Great Law of Love.

As we strive to become unified with God and learn to truly love one another, we need to constantly keep the four motives of life in balance. Everything that we do in our lives, from playing the guitar to programming computers to reading books to donating food to tickling our children, is done for one of four aims, motivations, goals or purposes. The four aims of life are:

- **Money**: your job, business, being able to pay the bills and have the ability to manifest on this Earth plane (which is ultimately all that money can do)

- **Pleasure**: recreation (re-creation), spending time with what we find to be beautiful and delightful

- **Service**: making the world a better place

- **God**: the personal pursuit of infinite truth—our "spiritual" life

We need to maintain all four of these motives in balance, or we cannot be a completely healthy person. Think of these four aims of life as being the four cylinders of the engine that is your soul. You need to have all four cylinders balanced and working together, or else your engine will be seriously hampered.

Or you could look at these four aims of life as legs on your animating soul. We want all four legs to be healthy.

These four motives/aims of life do *not* focus on *what* we are doing but upon our *reasons* for doing it. For example, let's take playing the guitar:

- **Money**: You could be playing the guitar for money (if you're good enough to be paid!).

- **Pleasure**: You could play the guitar simply as relaxation because you love the sound.

- **Service**: You might be playing the guitar at a nursing home to bring a little light to an otherwise drab existence.

- **God**: You could be playing the guitar as your form of meditation or prayer, seeking communion with the Divine.

The aims of life are not bound to any particular activity because any activity could be done for any one of the four motives. It's a question of what you're trying to accomplish.

Money

In the New Testament, Jesus speaks more about money than he does about heaven. Paul says, "If one does not work, do not let them eat."[1] Even those who are seriously handicapped can find *something* they can do to contribute to society. We need to reawaken an appreciation and respect for *all* kinds of labor, and everyone must be encouraged to find something they can do to support themselves and the economy of the family, community and world.

Some things we do for money are fun, and some can be very mundane, but *all* work provides an important balance and service in life.

All work is to be honored, as long as it is honorable.

It is best to find a job or career in a business that reflects who and what you are because if you are building bombs during the day, you're going to find it difficult to be a whole person and serve love with the rest of your time. We need to find and create businesses, jobs and professions that reflect who and what we are as loving, spirit-filled human beings.

Pleasure

Jesus was not afraid to drink a little wine, and when things became too hectic, he would remove himself from the insanity of the maddening crowds. He found restoration in quiet, safe places. In order for us to taste the joys and beauty of life, it is absolutely essential for us to find ways to relax, re-create and restore our souls. When we obsess about our jobs, work long hours away from the family or overdo in any aspect of our lives, we are in danger of becoming out of balance and losing our souls.

---

[1] NT Second Thessalonians 3:10

Service

It has been made plain to the Future Testament staff that, year in and year out, service to others is the one aspect of Christian life that most are missing. In our modern mechanized societies, we do our jobs, spend time on recreation, and even attend devotional activities, but spend relatively little of our time actually helping our fellow human beings.

Just as everyone has an ability to help the social order through work, everyone has talents and skills they can use to help a brother or sister in need. Social service is a fundamental cornerstone in defining what it means to be a human being. Too many of us live in isolation, mesmerized by our various media, attending to our private "spirituality" (which is no genuine spirituality at all). We pretend that we are "spiritual but not religious," yet all we really accomplish is to celebrate our own "I, me, mine" narcissism at the expense of our fellow humans and our own soul.

God

This motivation is prayer, meditation, singing praise, chanting the Name, reading and research—whatever it is that you do to come closer to the Divine. The Future Testament stresses the need for you to make your religion your own. To simply accept the religion of your parents and society without thought or reflection, and without making it your own, is akin to having no religion at all.

Balance and Cooperation

As citizens of the world, we must spend time contributing to the social order in business and money, focusing on our own relaxation, serving the needs of others *and* searching for God

It is essential that we keep these four aims in balance. At no point in your life should any one of these four aims occupy less than 10% (one tenth) of your time, nor more than 50% (half) of your time. Certainly, there are times and seasons for everything, and you may be called to work extended hours for a few weeks or even months. You might work 60-80 hours this week, but you cannot sustain such a work schedule on a permanent basis because such a schedule endangers your body, mind and soul.

Generally, on a week-by-week basis,

- We should spend no more than 50 hours a week on the job and no less than 10 hours a week on the job.

- We should spend no more than 50 hours a week and no less than 10 hours a week on recreation.

- We should spend no more than 50 hours a week helping others. If all you are doing is serving others, you are also in danger of losing your own soul. Still, we should spend no less than 10 hours a week on an average basis in our efforts to make the world a better place.

- Likewise, we should never spend more than 50 hours a week searching for God. Those who dedicate themselves exclusively to the quest for God are off the path and are not whole people. However, we should never spend less than 10 hours a week in our quest for the divine through prayer, meditation, singing songs of praise, etc.

Please notice the important way in which these four cylinders of the engine of the soul *work together*. In a four-cylinder engine, it is the other three cylinders that work to compress the gas, generate the explosion, continuing to the next cycle. In similar fashion, *each of the four aims of life greatly enhances the others*!

- **Money**. While it is true that the love of money is the root of all kinds of evil,[1] having money enables you to have more options in your pursuit of the other three aims. The more money you have, the more time you can spend in the quality recreations that you really value. The more money you have, the more you are able to fund those causes that help other human beings. If you have a healthy business, are not in debt and are not relying on others for your support, you have the peace of mind, the focus and the time to be able to pursue the Divine.

- **Pleasure**. Likewise, if you regularly spend time relaxing, involved in recreation and finding pleasure in life, you are renewed when it comes time to return to business, and your heart is refreshed when it comes time to serve other human beings who are hurting. Being relaxed and renewed gives you

---

[1] NT First Timothy 6:10, Hebrews 13:5

a heart that can rejoice and, with gratitude, seek for the Divine source of all.

- **Service**. If you're out making the world a better place, you will very often come in contact with opportunities to create new relationships with people that will help your business. Helping others can be a great source of pleasure as we discover new friends and new avenues for love. And when we truly look into the eyes of a stranger and clearly hear the cries of a child, we find the Face of God.

- **God**. A healthy spiritual life focused on seeking for God will find the other three aims ever more fulfilling. You will find a job that helps you to express your spirituality, or you will find new ways of seeing your present job as a ministry. The balanced spiritual life brings honor, honesty, integrity and concentration to the job, making you a much more successful business person. A God-touched life is able to appreciate the sacred nature of pleasure. Through the love of God, we find love for all of humanity, a love that will inspire us to make the world a better place.

God is interested in the balanced whole of you. God knows the totality you came here to be. The Old, New and Future Testaments want to raise you up in every aspect, so that you become that balanced whole.

Still, because you are free, it remains up to you to make sure that every day, week and month you are attending to all four aims of life: the garden of your soul.

In terms of *practical applications,* we know of no other discipline that has near the power for optimized health that a concentrated dedication to the Four Aims of Life does.

Church

A functional church, local, national or global, *must* properly balance the Four Aims of Life:

- **Money**. We must be wise stewards of our money. There is so much that could be said about this. Lavish spending and piles of debt, all in the so-called name of God, never serve the kingdom.

- **Pleasure**. Church should be *fun*. Interesting music, laughter, fellowship, meals… It's supposed to be a family, and joyous, folks.

- **Service**. Always remember that we are here to Love our fellow brothers and sisters as ourselves. That should be enough said.

- **God**. Study, prayer, communion…

And it should be more than obvious how all four of these work together to enhance each other, as they do for us personally.

Beyond individuals and churches, every family and business ideally would encompass the Four Aims of Life.

But, at this stage of human development, we are getting *way* ahead of ourselves here(!)

Supplement 3: Resacralization

The Future Testament tells of many cycles, such as freedom and knowledge and the Breath of God. We will now consider the cycle of the sacred.

Consider the Sun. We begin in total ignorance: we see the Sun, feel the warm rays and are overwhelmed with the magic of the beautiful golden orb. This ignorance causes us to consider the Sun sacred, and we worship it. We create rituals, songs and entire religions dedicated to the Sun.

As our cycle progresses, we become more knowledgeable, more scientifically aware of how the Sun works. We discover how hydrogen and helium and plasma create energy, light, radio waves and heat. And precisely at that point, we very often lose our wonder. What began as magic has become mundane. The Sun need no longer be worshiped as a god because it is "just" different atoms undergoing chemical exchanges.

Often the dawn of recognition brings contempt.

The same cyclic process has happened with our attitude toward life. Early humankind considered every single birth to be a transcendent miracle. Now that we understand the structure of DNA and have learned to perform in vitro fertilization, life has been cheapened. Birth has become a medical procedure to be performed at the convenience of the medical staff, and the new life that begins becomes a number before she even leaves the hospital.

The miraculous is no longer even worthy of note… except to those with eyes to see.

Make Sacred Again

"Resacralization" is a lovely word that means "to make sacred again." Resacralization is intimately connected to the aspiration of the Future Testament, which is to

- reunite the sacred and the mundane,

- reunite religion and science,

- reunite the pathways of heart and mind and

- reunite reason and faith.

Early humankind witnessed birth and saw the Sun, and it found the miraculous. To be in awe and wonder is the pathway of the heart, the pathway of faith.

Initially, everything is sacred, from the rocks to the trees, the wind and the sky and rain: it is all sacred. It is all inside God.[1] To consider the miraculous wonder of rain provides a window into the supernatural gift that is water from the sky. Wizards and witches, gods and goddesses, angels and demons, fairies and elves can be imagined inhabiting everything, and we see with eyes of curiosity much like the children we used to be.

Finding the sacred in all life gives way to scientific reason: rationality reigns, and suddenly God turns into chemicals, formulas and scientific properties. The world no longer seems to be a sacred place when it has become a series of molecules that happen to interact in intriguing ways.

When we complete the cycle, *both* the initial impulse of worshiping the Universe *and* the later impulse of rationally understanding it will be united!

Each shall be enhanced by the other.

The heart now knows *why* it is so in love.

Considering the Sun… we now know it is 93 million miles away, has a mass of 2×10^{30} kilograms and burns 10 million tons every second… Our original religious devotion, born of ignorance and fear, can be resacralized, reborn of understanding and enlightened goodness.

As we pursue our sciences far enough, we will realize that, though we may be able to understand the Sun, zygotes, DNA, fertilization and birth… that does not mean that any of these is less than miraculous!

Notice the ways in which resacralization is directly connected to our previous topic, in which we discussed how your business, pleasure, service and quest for God all need to be united. The Future Testament emphasizes in many different ways that the heart of faith and the mind

---

[1] NT Acts 17:28

of rationality must be reunited and work together. Science and religion must celebrate their reunion for the human race to take the next steps toward the stars.

The religious people who *say* they "love God and that's all they need to know," then throw their sacred lives away with television or gossip or any other banality, have no true love or appreciation for God. The most devout Christians should be the most rabid scientists, seeking to learn everything there is to know about the miraculous nature of God's creation. This is why the Future Testament counsels you to learn everything about everything: mathematics, chemistry, biology, physics, biochemistry, psychology, history, scripture, literature—*there is no aspect of life or truth that should be ignored or considered to be unimportant.*

We are seeing scientists who began their careers as confirmed atheists; they discover complexities and wonders of the mathematical, chemical, physical and astronomical Universes that utterly astound them; they are forced to accept their own resacralization of the Universe.

Through a secular pursuit of the mind, their hearts realize the transcendent presence of what we call God.

The heart will lead us to the mind; the mind will lead us to the heart.

Science will lead us to religion; religion will lead us to science. The two currently seem to be at odds, and it may look as though their differences are irreconcilable, but that is not true. Divergent notions in science and religion about "creation" and "evolution" will eventually become one truth. "I am the truth. No one comes to the Father but by me."[1] No one approaches God except through truth.

When we really know the *full* truth of what life is, science will be religious, and our religion will be scientific. The two shall become one. Not one *flesh,* but one system.[2]

The process of resacralization pertains to everything in your life. It is one thing to say "Oh, it's just dinner." But with a moment of spoken or silent gratitude, recognizing the truly glorious and miraculous way your food came to *be,* dinner becomes a sacred event. Even the most mundane activities become glorious expressions of the Divine. Through following the four aims of life, work becomes a sacred

---

[1] NT John 14:6
[2] FT Liberty 1:3

function, recreation becomes a way of seeing God, serving our fellow human beings becomes a way to build relationships and create a better world, and seeking God becomes the supreme pleasure of life; all four aims work together. The four are not one *flesh,* but one *system.*

The reunification of our fractured consciousness will lead us to a resacralized world where *everything* is seen as a sacred gift, even those things which may seem "bad," because even (especially!) the "bad" things give us the opportunity to heal, to serve and to extend love to all of God's children.

Supplement 4:
The Ancestral Testaments

The world is vast, confusing and frightening. How should we live? Which way should we go? And, most importantly, *how do I know?*

It is certainly understandable that people want a norm, a guide, an infallible source they can turn to for guidance through life. And for millions, that infallible source is the Bible, Old and New Testaments.

Sitting every Sunday in your normal pew, it's easy to get the idea that we have the original writings of Saint Peter, Saint Paul and Luke the physician locked in a vault somewhere.

We don't.

It's easy to get the impression that God dropped the Holy Scriptures out of heaven complete and ready to go.

He didn't.

Until you actually study the matter, it's easy to think that the apostles got together and decided which were going to be the writings for the New Testament, and the matter was settled in a couple of days.

It wasn't.

The truth of the matter is very far removed from these simplified notions. Many people are astounded and somewhat disturbed as they research how the Bible came to be:

- We do not have, anywhere, the original writings by anyone involved in the Bible.

- We do not have a single scrap of writing, in any form, that bears Saint Paul's, Peter's or Isaiah's actual handwriting.

- In fact, most of the documents that are in existence are *hundreds of years separated* from the time of their writing.

- Saint Paul probably never read the letters of Peter.

- The writer of Luke's Gospel probably never read First or Second John.

- Most of the Biblical books were originally letters written and passed around to different churches. Some letters became very popular, and it was their popularity that made them significant enough to be retained as Christianity developed from a fledgling, upstart religion into the official religion of Rome.

- The process by which it was finally determined which 39 books would be in the Old Testament and which 27 would be in the New Testament took *hundreds of years*. Different groups liked some books and disliked others. There were arguments and factions as to which books would and would not be considered to be "holy."

- What is more, there were many, *many* additional writings that didn't "make the cut" for the final authoritative list we now call the "canon." There were numerous other epistles written. There were other Gospels written, too: the Gospel of Thomas and the Gospel of Mary, among others.

- So it isn't as if a few variations of the 27 books of the New Testament were the only documents from which the New Testament could be created: there are literally *scores* of other significant writings that were finally *voted out*.

Don't ever doubt that's what happened: the final, authoritative contents of the Bible were determined by *vote*, *hundreds* of years after Jesus' life and death. And resurrection.

Over the years, different early Christian factions were warring against one another, and finally the civil authorities demanded everyone get together and decide by final *vote* as to which documents would or would not be the authoritative works to be taught to Christians throughout the centuries.

The epistles, Gospels and other documents that were rejected came to be considered unworthy, even an abomination, and were discarded. The only documents worthy to be taught to our children and our children's children were those agreed upon by *vote*.

The Future Testament strongly suggests that you look into the matter of the formation of the canon for yourself. You will see that the formation took hundreds of years and involved thousands of people in a process which can only be called political compromise.

Why does any of this matter? It matters because many people today think as though the Old and New Testaments literally fell out of heaven and were delivered to them by the very hand of God.

It did not happen that way.

Different writings from different people in different areas had different popularity from other groups until finally, ecumenical councils (the equivalent of our modern political parties) sat down and *voted* on the final list, hundreds of years after the event. Many of the documents were written in languages the people of the day didn't even speak. Jesus didn't even speak the language the Gospels are written in!

The formation of the canon from our ancestral documents was much more human-involved than the average parishioner understands. Some people want to believe that God "channeled" these writings, which led to the notion that these particular books are somehow inerrant and perfect. People like to believe that God wrote them somehow, and every single word is therefore mathematically, scientifically, spiritually and psychologically perfect. In our crazy world, this perceived literal perfection of the Bible is one thing to be counted on as "trustworthy."

It is not remotely that simple.

The Old, New and Future Testaments are infused with humanity, works written by very human beings at a very specific time with very specific backgrounds, dreams and hopes for the future.

This is not bad—it is wonderful!

Nothing here is to disparage the Bible. We should all celebrate its glorious birth and the truths it contains. The Bible is a sacred recording of the lives of hundreds of people searching for God, finding the highest truth they could know and documenting their history in the best way they could.

It fits perfectly with the recipe, experience and community aspects of verifiable knowledge!

As they searched and struggled for God, God did indeed inspire and touch them. Once again we can see the process of unification: in the incarnation, we see Jesus as fully God and fully man. So too, in the formation of the canon, we can see the Divine and the human being unified.

These scriptural writings tell of human beings reaching for God, and when God was able to get through to us, He communicated eternal truths. As the Future Testament makes clear, we must distinguish the eternal, infinite truth of God from the temporary cultural truth of humankind. Where those lines are drawn is what separates liberals from conservatives and Orthodox from Reformed.

The point is that the scriptures of the Old, New and Future Testaments are very human documents, written by people, in their quest for God.

With research into the rejected scriptures, only *you* can determine if the books that were included were the "right" books. Maybe the ecumenical counsels were wrong, and the Gospel of Mary belongs in your canon.

> **Please note this carefully: in different places, the Bible quotes writings that are called *scripture*, but such writings *cannot be found in the Bible!***

In the Gospel of John, for example, Jesus is quoted as saying "As the *scripture* says, from his innermost being will flow streams of living water."[1] Jesus calls the statement *scripture*, yet *it cannot be found anywhere in the Old or New Testaments.*

In other words, the Bible declares that the Son of God quoted what he considered to be sacred scripture, but *what he quoted cannot be found in our current Bible.*

James, the brother of Jesus, says, "Do you think that the scripture speaks to no purpose: 'He jealously desires the spirit which he has made to dwell in us'?"[2] But this "scripture" appears nowhere in the Old or New Testament!

Jude, traditionally another brother of Jesus, quotes extensively from Enoch, the seventh generation from Adam.[3] The only tiny problem is that his almost 50-word quote cannot be found anywhere in the Old or New Testament.

---

[1] NT John 7:38
[2] NT James 4:5
[3] NT Jude 1:14 & 15

Often the publishers of New Testament translations are desperate to hide these discrepancies. The unknown author of Hebrews quotes the Old Testament with

"And let all the angels of God worship Him."[1]

The editors of the New American Standard, with a tiny note in the margin, say this is a quote of

"Rejoice, O nations, with his people,
    for he will avenge the blood of his servants;
  he will render vengeance on his adversaries
      and will atone for his land and His people."[2]

Most people can see that the Old Testament passage quoted shows *no resemblance* to what the New Testament quotes!

Likewise, Paul claims the following is written in scripture:

"No eye has seen,
  no ear has heard,
  no mind has conceived
what God has prepared for those who love him."[3]

The best the Bible editors can come up with is to say this is a quote from Isaiah:

"Since ancient times no one has heard,
  no ear has perceived,
  no eye has seen any God besides you,
who acts on behalf of those who wait for him."[4]

In fact, Paul is quoting a book that is not in the Bible.

---

[1] NT Hebrews 1:6
[2] OT Deuteronomy 32:43
[3] NT First Corinthians 2:9
[4] OT Isaiah 64:4

Paul quotes some Roman poets as saying, "For we also are his offspring."[1] Here, secular, "pagan" authors have their writings declared *scripture* because Paul quotes them, thus placing them in the "real" scripture!

Are there, perhaps, other "secular" authors we should consider sacred?!

What other writings did Jesus consider sacred? What other Roman pagan authors wrote divinely inspired works?

Please be clear. The holy, inspired, perfect, inerrant Word of God (as it is worshipped by millions) quotes, *as scripture*, books that were voted out of the Bible. In addition, it quotes Roman pagans, who wrote something so true that it had to be included in the New Testament.

This is a profound mystery that is also incredibly exciting because it means that *you too* are offered the opportunity to find the sacred outside of what an ecclesiastical voting structure declared to be scripture!

You are invited to freely participate in the formation of your own canon.

Centuries after the final canonization of the Bible, Martin Luther wanted to throw some of the books out. Luther wanted to get rid of the Book of James and eliminate the Book of Revelation. Martin Luther was not afraid to find scripture where he found inspiration from God.

Jesus, James and Paul called scripture where they found it, even when it was not in the Bible!

You are invited to do the same. Please see the Future Testament, **The Book of Scripture.**

For Further Reading

We recommend "*The Biblical Canon: Its Origin, Transmission, and Authority*" by Lee Martin McDonald, © 2007, Hendrickson Publishers, Peabody, Massachusetts.

---

[1] NT Acts 17:28

Supplement 5:
Beyond Biblical Inerrancy

As we said in the previous supplement, people want to believe that the Bible was written by the hand of God and descended on clouds out of heaven, accompanied by angels. People very often want to believe that what is written in the Bible is absolutely true. Inerrant. Perfect.

The desire for perfect scripture is certainly understandable. The world is confusing and frightening. We face moral dilemmas that are soul-wrenching and financial, technological and environmental challenges so astoundingly complex they seem impossible to solve. As a species, humanity faces problems at every front.

In the face of such terrible uncertainty, we think it would be nice to have a guide to tell us precisely where to go and what to do. Sometimes people will turn to a psychic or a fortune-teller or look to astrological readings. Some live by their gut feelings, others look for an authority figure who will tell them what to do, and others wait for dreams and visions. The list is long.

Many people turn to a holy book, wishfully thinking, "this book is perfect—all I have to do is follow what's in this book, and I will be fine."

The more you really know, the more you realize it is only wishful thinking.

Small Matters

Many people espouse that the Bible is literally and inerrantly the word of God, without contradiction, blemish or flaw because if God wrote it, of course there could be no mistakes.

Others will talk about "Bible errors" and point to minor problems in the text. Read literally, the Bible would seem to indicate that the value of pi is 3, not the much more precise 3.14159265... that we know is the scientific truth.[1] Taken literally, the Bible would seem to indicate that

---

[1] OT First Kings 7:23 and 26, Second Chronicles 4: 2 - 5

rabbits chew their cud, but they don't.[1] Many will go to *extreme lengths* to explain away these issues, often to the point of absurdity. Depending on your perspective, there are potentially dozens of such issues in the Old and New Testaments.

But these silly arguments are futile and serve no purpose:

- Those who believe the Bible is literally true will claim that such mistakes are because of a translation error, or they will use any number of devices to explain away the apparent "problem."

- On the other hand, those who wish to hate the Bible will use these apparent misunderstandings as reason to find it valueless and throw away the whole book. They will use such inconsistencies as a reason to excuse the Bible from their lives.

The Future Testament finds both positions rather silly and extreme.

Let us consider the account of Jesus' resurrection as an example. If you carefully read the accounts of Jesus' resurrection from each of the Gospels, you will find what, to many people, appear to be contradictions. Exactly who was at the tomb? How many angels were there? When and to whom did the angels appear? Some people will say that the Gospels contradict one another. Others will go to great lengths to declare there are no contradictions whatsoever and all the Gospel stories fit perfectly well together.

Again, for the Future Testament team, such arguments are meaningless.

- If someone sees an apparent contradiction in the Bible, they can use it to say the Bible has no value. That's ridiculous.

- Likewise, if every single account matched to the letter, people could easily claim that the Gospel writers were clearly copying one another, and the stories couldn't be genuine eyewitness accounts—and discount the entire Bible on that basis!

- Other people, upon noticing these minor contradictions, feel quite certain that these were *genuine* eyewitness accounts by real people because no one remembers events exactly as others do. For these people, the minor inconsistencies help to

---

[1] OT Leviticus 11:6

reinforce the notion that the Bible can be trusted in its account of Jesus' resurrection from death.

Notice that the actual details simply don't matter. Whether the Bible *does* or *does not* contain contradictions, *is* or *is not* literally and mathematically perfect in everything it says, can be used by either side to reach either conclusion:

- If there are contradictions in the Bible, to some that means it should be thrown away, while to others the contradictions establish its veracity.

- If the Bible is mathematically perfect without contradiction, to some that means it is divinely written, but to others it means collusion, and therefore the Bible is useless.

The discussion is meaningless. Any and all arguments about the inerrancy of scripture resolve themselves as trivialities.

Matters that Matter

The Future Testament authors want you to know that far beyond the trivial matters of scientific or alleged eyewitness contradictions, there is much deeper disagreement within the scriptures and between the different writers.

Much of the Bible fundamentally argues with other parts of the Bible.

As the Jewish people quested for God and looked for what was real, many of the important issues and cultural dilemmas of the day were addressed, argued over and changed in the Bible. It is not a matter of minor inconsistencies and contradictions: it's that *the Bible argues with itself over what is true*! The Future Testament finds this to be exciting, because it shows that the authors were truly searching for God and truth and were not afraid to find other parts of their scripture wanting adjustment, if need be.

For example, as you read Genesis, Exodus, Leviticus, Numbers and Deuteronomy, you will find long discussions about exactly how different sacrifices are supposed to be performed. These were not trivial matters to the early Hebrew people: sacrifice was integral to their worship. At the turn of the 21st century, some are even seeking to reestablish the blood sacrifices in Israel.

However, the Book of Hosea makes the following very bold statement: "For I delight in loyalty *rather than sacrifice*, and in the knowledge of God *rather than burnt offerings*."[1] The entire series of Hebrew sacrifices and rituals were called into question.

Huge amounts of time and effort were used by the Hebrews to build the temple, a "house" for God, and yet we see in Isaiah, "This is what Yahweh says:

"Heaven is my throne,
and the Earth is my footstool.
Where is the house you will build for me?
Where will my resting place be?
Has not my hand made all these things,
and so they came into being?"
declares Yahweh.[2]

And, continuing with the condemnation of the sacrificial system, that same passage in Isaiah continues,

"This is the one I esteem:
he who is humble and contrite in spirit,
and trembles at my word.
But whoever sacrifices a bull
is like one who kills a man,
and whoever offers a lamb,
like one who breaks a dog's neck;
whoever makes a grain offering
is like one who presents pig's blood,
and whoever burns memorial incense,
like one who worships an idol.
They have chosen their own ways,
and their souls delight in their abominations."[3]

Moses said that a man can simply say, "I divorce you," and be done with his wife, but Jesus said it was never supposed to be that way from the beginning.[4]

---

[1] OT Hosea 6:6
[2] OT Isaiah 66:1 - 2
[3] OT Isaiah 66:2 - 3
[4] NT Matthew 19:7

The repudiation of Mosaic Law, the ritual sacrifices and the temple worship were the most significant issues of Jewish religious life. These are far from trivial differences. But this is just the beginning.

Have you ever read Psalm 137? It is very clear. From the modern translation: "O Babylon, how blessed will be those who dash your little babies' heads against the rock."[1] Psalm 137, from the Holy Word of God, says that the Jewish people will find a *blessing* if they smash the heads of their captor's (Babylon) babies against a rock. The verse actually states that God will bless such killing of innocents. Jesus, however, makes it very plain that we are to "Love your enemies, do good to those who hate you, bless those who curse you, pray for those who mistreat you."[2] That is a far cry from receiving a blessing for crushing a baby's skull with a rock, don't you think? Jesus put his life behind his every word. As he hung upon the cross, Jesus said, "Father, forgive them for they know not what they do."[3]

The Truth of God

Serving and loving God is not simply a matter of covering your head or never cutting your hair,[4] or even of circumcising your male children.

Rather, to know, love and serve God encompasses all of what it means to be a human being here in the world, what it means to love and serve and forgive.

Inerrancy? Real scripture is so much more than that. God moves from being a God of vengeance and war in the Old Testament to being a God of loving and forgiving, regardless of the cost, in the New Testament. We have tried to continue this pattern of growth in the Future Testament.

The Bible is a precious record of humanity's quest to find out what is true. If the ways of old are found to be false or mistaken, it is time to find a new way!

You are invited to do the same thing. Whether they are found in the Old, New or Future Testaments, if the old ways are found to be wanting or out of alignment with your mind's understanding and your heart's

---

[1] OT Psalm 137: 8 - 9
[2] NT Luke 6:28 - 29
[3] NT Luke 23:34
[4] NT First Corinthians 11:6

love for God, *it is your spiritual obligation to make corrections for yourself.* Create a new recipe. Experience Love. And share it with the world. Far beyond the question of inerrancy lies the quest for Divinity, as humanity reaches for its destiny.

Supplement 6:
God's Name Yahweh

In the Jewish and Christian traditions, there is only one personal Name for God. There is much folklore about this Name, including superstitions. There is also a lot of confusion. There is much that can be said about the Name, and we invite you to see our recommendation at the end of this supplement for much more information.

But for the purposes of the Future Testament, this much you must know.

Moses asks God what His name is, and God says,

> **"I Will Be what I Will Be... This is My memorial Name forever."**[1]

This may be new or shocking to you. We usually see the Name translated as "I Am." While "I Am that I Am" certainly has value, it is ultimately a mistranslation, a Christian interpretation applied 1,000 years after the fact.

When Moses came down the mountain, the people asked him what God's Name was. Moses dutifully said, "I Will Be what I Will Be." This made people very nervous.[2] Why? Well, they heard Moses say, "*I Will Be.*" That sounded like blasphemy to them.

So, God's innermost personal Name, "I Will Be what I Will Be," (Ehyeh Asr Ehyeh) was changed. The final version, known as the Tetragrammaton, the "four-letter Name," appears in the Bible as God's personal Name over 6,100 times.

No one *really* knows how the Tetragrammaton was derived. Most scholars consider it to be a combination of "He Was," "He Is" and "He Will Be."

---

[1] OT Exodus 3:14

[2] You will not find this in the Old or New Testaments. It is a part of the vast tradition of Jewish commentaries on the Bible.

In Hebrew (spelled right to left), the Tetragrammaton Name looks like this:

These four letters, right to left, are

a Yod, rhymes with "rode," which we transliterate "Y"

a Heh, rhymes with "say," which we transliterate "H"

a Vav, like "lava," which we transliterate "W" or "V"

another Heh

No one knows exactly what Moses heard from the burning bush. So no one knows exactly how to pronounce this Name. This is one of the things that people love to argue about with great vehemence, claiming they *do* know the original pronunciation, when it is simply not possible.

So, a wide variety of pronunciations are known. Some spell the letters, like saying "F-B-I," as "Yod-Heh-Vav-Heh." Some say "yah-VEY." Others "YAH-way." Even "Jehovah" comes from the Tetragrammaton, though there is no "J" sound in ancient Hebrew.

Originally, Hebrew did not have vowels. So, the transliteration of "Yod-Heh-Vav-Heh" is

YHWH

Honoring the importance of the Tetragrammaton, the Future Testament spells The Name as

Yahweh

We use "Yahweh" for God's Name throughout the text, and we actually pronounce it "Yod-Heh-Vav-Heh" in our circles. But you are free to use whatever pronunciation is comfortable to you.

Acknowledging people's common use of language (and, after all, that's what a language is: how people use it), the Future Testament uses

"God" and "Yahweh" interchangeably, as in "God did this" or "Yahweh did that." But please be clear: "God" is a noun, *what* the Divine *is.* "Yahweh" is the Name of God.

If you go looking for Yahweh or YHWH in your Bible, you will probably not find it. What you will find, over 6,100 times, is "LORD" in all caps. The tradition developed, due to superstition, that saying or writing the Divine Tetragrammaton could bring a curse on you if you had any sin. So, over many centuries, the tradition developed to replace "YHWH" with "LORD."

But this much we know for certain. The Tetragrammaton is God's *personal* Name and points to God's *real* Name. Amazingly, when the Tetragrammaton is spelled vertically, it forms a pictogram of a human being:

This is a visual representation of what it symbolically means to be created in the image of God.[1]

So, for your deep meditation, learn the parable of The Name: You relate to your name as God relates to you.

You are God's *real* Name, which is symbolized by His *personal* Name, the Tetragrammaton.

For Further Reading

For more information, we recommend visiting www.Yhwh.com.

---

[1] OT Genesis 1:26

Supplement 7:
Truth in Embryo

The Future Testament relies on the notion of truth in embryo as one of the keys to greater spiritual understanding. Sometimes people outside (and inside) the church find certain religious or scriptural ideas to be silly.

One example we have used is the notion of the Trinity expressed as three persons making up one God, a very difficult doctrine to justify. But when you see the triune (three in one) nature of every single relationship everywhere in the Universe, the notion of God as a Trinity becomes one of the most profound revelations a human being can possibly understand.

Subject and object are one in their relationship. From the largest perspectives to the smallest, from how governments and businesses work to how energy is shared at the subatomic level, the trinity is forever true. Since God is everywhere, for in God we live, move and exist, if God is a Trinity, then it is reasonable to expect we will find the trinity everywhere, and in fact, we do.

That's the notion behind truth in embryo. Before we discard an idea as being ridiculous or medieval, we need to make sure we're not being overly hasty. We need to understand *why* the idea developed and make certain that we have given the idea time to incubate in our minds and hearts before we throw it away.

Take the notion of communion: eating and drinking the body and blood of Jesus. For hundreds of millions of Christians around the globe, communion is the cornerstone of their religious life. On the other hand, for many inside and outside the church, communion is a disgusting notion. And yet, we know that nothing is ever created or destroyed; things only change form. Therefore, everything in the physical Universe is simply a portion of God that has been poured out and slowed down. Whenever we eat, then, we are literally eating the "body of God." When we take a glass of water, we are literally drinking God's "blood."

Perhaps you noticed that this idea is directly related to the notion of resacralization. Eating and drinking are sacred acts of worship.

Everything that we are is a part of God. Everything that we see is a part of God. Everything that we can touch, eat, drink, breathe or manipulate in any way is a part of God. Holy Communion is *every moment*. The idea of communion, eating and drinking the body and blood of one's god, is vastly older than Christianity, while at the same time, the full understanding of what it means to be consciously aware of taking in particles of God-stuff is still an idea in embryo.

In no way does the Future Testament seek to throw out any part of the Old or New Testaments without a very close and careful examination.

Many statements made in the Old and New Testaments have been found to be less than divine in the light of unconditional love, in the light of God as the perfectly loving parent or in the context of scientific or historical discovery. Such statements can then be lovingly placed in the category of temporal cultural traditions instead of the eternal truths of a loving God. Sublimating women to second-class status cannot he the real truth of God. Slavery of any kind cannot be the truth of God. The length of a person's hair or whether you worship God with your head covered cannot matter to God. One atoning vicariously for another cannot be the eternal truth. God wants each of us to grow into our own fruit of the Spirit and not depend on another's sacrifice as a substitute for our own growth and spiritual maturation.

Truth in embryo is a notion that is glorious to watch because ideas sometimes take centuries to completely develop. Now that the human race has discovered fractals and chaos theory, we are able to begin to see a small part of the glory of God's Holy Name, a name that appeared in the original Biblical record thousands of years ago. God's name, translated "I will be what I will be," is a fractal relationship. The output for one cycle of "I will be" becomes the input for the next cycle of "I will be."

Right there, in an ancient document, as God revealed His name to Moses, He was pointing toward the discovery of fractals and chaos theory in centuries to come.

Truth in embryo: you are encouraged to find eternal truth and let it grow. Let it become you, because you too are infinite truth.

You are God in embryo.

About the Authors

The authors of this document matter only in the way that all people do, as Divinity's Children. Their identities and backgrounds have no bearing on the text of the Future Testament.

The material here stands or falls on its own merit, as you examine and test it in terms of your own life.

Accepting any of the Future Testament simply because its authors have a background that you respect, or come from an organization you like, is a bad idea.

Likewise, rejecting anything here simply because of something in the authors' past makes no sense at all.

In short, the authors of the Future Testament do not matter.

Only the text of the Future Testament matters, and what it means to you.

Made in United States
North Haven, CT
27 March 2022

17595438R00136